ISSUES IN
SCIENCE AND THEOLOGY

ISSUES IN
SCIENCE AND THEOLOGY

This series is published under the auspices of the
European Society for the Study of Science and Theology (ESSSAT)

Editor

NIELS HENRIK GREGERSEN
Associate Professor of Systematic Theology
University of Aarhus, Denmark

Advisory Board

The Human Person
in Science and
Theology

The Human Person in Science and Theology

Editors

NIELS HENRIK GREGERSEN
WILLEM B. DREES
ULF GÖRMAN

T&T CLARK
EDINBURGH

T&T CLARK LTD
59 GEORGE STREET
EDINBURGH EH2 2LQ
SCOTLAND

www.tandtclark.co.uk

First published 2000

ISBN 0 567 08692 5

British Library Cataloguing-in-Publication Data
A catalogue record for this book is available from the British Library

Typeset by Waverley Typesetters, Galashiels
Printed and bound in Great Britain by Bell & Bain Ltd, Glasgow

Contents

PART II
SUPERVENIENCE, MIND AND CULTURE

Preface and Acknowledgments

This volume is the fruit of a joint effort of scholars in an exciting conversation between scientists, philosophers, and theologians. In this interdisciplinary area The European Society for the Study of Science and Theology (ESSSAT) aims to advance an open and critical communication between science and theology in order to achieve a mutual cross-fertilization of the disciplines and to work on the solution of interdisciplinary problems.

From 31 March to 5 April 1998 ESSSAT organized the Seventh European Conference on Science and Theology in Durham, UK, on the theme: 'The Person: Perspectives from Science and Theology.' Many participants sought to articulate an understanding of the human person as a bio-cultural reality. As essays in this volume make clear, one then enters a rich discussion on the implications of such an understanding of our own nature for religious life and theological thinking.

The present volume includes the plenary lectures of the conference in Durham, illuminating scientific, philosophical and theological aspects of 'the person'. Furthermore, the book offers a discussion on different versions of supervenience as a possible view of the intimate relation between brain, mind, and culture.

Studies in Science and Theology (*SSTh*) will publish as its Volume 7 another selection of papers presented at the conference, together with otherwise related contributions to the ongoing dialogue between science and theology.

The quality and dimension of a pan-European activity such as an ESSSAT conference is possible only through a number of sponsors. We express our gratitude to the John M. Templeton Foundation for its generous financial support which made it possible to invite distinguished scholars for the plenary lectures. Generous grants from the Renovabis Foundation and from the John M. Templeton Foundation have offered ESSSAT the possibility to support a number of participants from Eastern Europe with scholarships. Other sponsors of the conference were the AAAS Program for Dialogue between Science and Religion and the Theological Faculty at Lund University. ESSSAT wishes to express its deep gratitude to all the sponsors, as well as to Anne Marie Baden Olsen and Bente Stær at the Department of Systematic Theology, University of Aarhus, for their meticulous assistance with editing the manuscripts.

Last but not least we owe thanks to T&T Clark and the William B. Eerdmans Publishing Company for cooperating with ESSSAT in inaugurating the new series, *Issues in Science and Theology,* of which this is the first volume.

List of Contributors

DENNIS BIELFELDT is Associate Professor of Philosophy and Religion at South Dakota State University in Brookings, South Dakota, USA. He has published widely in theology and science, philosophy of religion, Luther studies, and systematic theology. He is currently working on downward causation and the problem of divine action.

NIELS HENRIK GREGERSEN is Associate Professor of Systematic Theology at the University of Aarhus, Denmark. He has published three books in theology and edited several volumes in science and theology, most recently *Rethinking Theology and Science* (with J. Wentzel van Huyssteen). He is a Vice-President of ESSSAT and a co-editor of *Studies in Science and Theology* and *Dansk Teologisk Tidsskrift*.

PHILIP HEFNER is Professor of Systematic Theology, The Lutheran School of Theology at Chicago, USA. He is Director of the Zygon Center for Religion and Science, Chicago, and editor of *Zygon: Journal of Religion and Science*. His most recent book is *The Human Factor. Evolution, Culture and Religion*.

HUGO LAGERCRANTZ is Professor of Pediatrics at the Karolinska Institut, Stockholm, Sweden, and Director of the Neonatal Programme at the Astrid Lindgren Children's Hospital. His research concerns the birth transition, respiratory control, sudden infant death syndrome and brain development. He has published about 200 scientific papers, is European chief editor for Pediatric Research, and a member of the Nobel Assembly for medicine.

MARY MIDGLEY is a philosopher with a special interest in the relation between humans and the rest of nature and also in the connection between science and religion. Till her retirement she was a Senior Lecturer in Philosophy at the University of Newcastle on Tyne, UK. Her books include *Beast and Man, Evolution As A Religion, Science As Salvation, Wickedness, The Ethical Primate* and (most recently) *Utopias, Dolphins and Computers.*

JOHN A. TESKE is Professor of Psychology at Elizabethtown College, Elizabethtown, Pennsylvania. More recently he has published on brain, mind, and spirituality in *Studies in Science and Theology* and *Zygon,* and he co-edited the July 1999 issue of *Science and Spirit* on 'Mind, Morals and Evolution'.

REVD DR FRASER WATTS started his academic career as a psychologist and spent several years working in the Cambridge Applied Psychology Unit. For the last six years he has been the Starbridge Lecturer in Theology and Natural Science at the University of Cambridge. He has a special interest in the dialogue between theology and the human sciences, and recently edited *Science Meets Faith.*

MICHAEL WELKER is Professor of Systematic Theology and Director of Internationales Wissenschaftsforum at the University of Heidelberg. Recent publications include *God the Spirit, Creation and Reality,* and *What Happens in Holy Communion?* He has edited *Toward the Future of Reformed Theology* (with D. Willis) and *The End of the World and the Ends of God* (with John Polkinghorne). He is co-editor of *Evangelische Theologie, Soundings,* and *Journal of Law and Religion.*

1

Varieties of Personhood: Mapping the Issues

NIELS HENRIK GREGERSEN

I am a person. You, the reader of these lines, are a person too. Such statements merely express that we both are human beings. When a child shouts angrily at her parents, 'I am a person, too!', she is making a stronger statement. She might want to make clear that her feelings deserve to be respected even if they are quite different from the feelings of her parents. In states of coma, by contrast, doctors, care-givers and friends might wonder whether a patient 'is still a person'. The heart is still functioning, breathing goes on, but 'something' that made this human being a person seems to have been lost. What is this 'something'? What is the significance of being a person?

Apparently, the word 'person' is used in a variety of contexts and acquires a diversity of meanings as one goes from one discourse system into another. In colloquial conversation the word may be used to underline uniqueness, or the need for becoming a person in one's own right. In public discussions on ethics and legal issues attention is given to the rights and duties that we ascribe to persons as moral subjects. In all contexts, however, a human person is seen as a subject who deserves moral protection. Therefore, it hardly surprises that the concept of personhood plays a prominent role in disciplines such as bioethics, law, and political science as well as in philosophy and theology.

1

The notion of the human person is multifaceted, yet one characteristic feature reappears. In his *Concepts of Person and Christian
Ethics*, Stanley Rudman has convincingly shown how discussions
about persons consistently blend descriptive and prescriptive
elements. 'Person' is never a purely neutral term, but always a
description loaded with interests. 'At least since the nineteenth
century, but particularly in recent years, "persons" have come to
occupy a position of unparalleled regard in the competing value-
systems of pluralist societies', says Rudman (Rudman 1997, 3).
Everybody wants to be recognized as a person and everybody
strives to become 'one's own person', but what constitutes a person
has become highly contested.

The historical career of the term shows the extent to which the
notion of 'person' is socially conditioned. The questions are, first,
is it still a useful term that catches important features of what it
means to be human, and second, is it possible to correlate a
scientific view of human beings with an understanding of ourselves
as persons.

What Is a Person:
Individualistic versus Relational Views

The idea of a human person rests on Stoic and Christian notions of
humanity. Human persons share in a common rationality; therefore, they are legally accountable agents. Yet persons also possess
uniqueness as individuals. This idea of personhood reached its
heyday in modernity when *inner* subjectivity was emphasized. It
was claimed that a person had an inherent moral dignity. In the
early seventeenth century, Thomas Hobbes still underlined the old
practical sense in which a person is one 'to whom one can ascribe
human words and deeds' (*On Human Nature* 15). At the end of the
seventeenth century, John Locke defined a person as 'a thinking
intelligent Being, that has reason and reflection, and can consider
it self as it self, the same thinking thing in different times and
places' (*An Essay Concerning Human Understanding* II.27.9). Here
the notion of the individual as a reasoned self-identity is highlighted. Locke, however, pointed out that the feeling of personal

unity depends on a flow of discrete states of awareness held together by the glue of memory. The person thus constitutes a unity out of the diversity of the states of consciousness. Finally, Immanuel Kant, at the end of the eighteenth century, pointed to the co-presence of theoretical and practical rationality as the distinguishing mark of personhood. Moreover, without much argument, he believed that these human capacities for reasoning provide the basis for the 'absolute value' of human persons. Hence, everyone should be treated as an 'end in itself', never just as an instrument to some other purpose (*Foundations to a Metaphysics of Morals*, German original edn 1785, 65–71).

Thus in early modernity, we find a coalescence of the practical and the theoretical aspects of personhood, centering on the idea of individual autonomy. This early modern concept of personhood then paved the way for the concentration on the interiority of human beings which flourished with the existentialist and personalist philosophies of the twentieth century. In an anti-materialist sentiment, being a person and being a thing were now considered to be opposites. In consequence, philosophical treatments of personhood had nothing to with scientific descriptions of the human being.

More recently, the modern emphasis on interiorized autonomy has been challenged from many sides. Some non-Westerners see it as a biased Christian construct. Conservatives of various kinds (including Christian conservatives) criticize the idea of freedom as a 'liberal' concept that tends to undermine the communities which nurtured the self in the first place and continue to situate the self in a realm of values. Finally, postmodernists regard the idea of self-identity as a latch on a concept of 'monadic sameness' that remains 'immune to the rancor of temporal becoming' (Schrag 1997, 53).

Current debates about the limits of 'personal autonomy' and cultural constraints of 'human rights' can thus be seen as signals of a growing dissatisfaction with the tendency to identify person and privacy. Should one always give priority to the individual capacities of the human person, or should one rather emphasize that one is always a person in a web of relations? In the first case, *autonomy* is regarded as a prime characteristic of personhood. In the latter case, *relationality* is underlined and selves are seen as situated in families, communities and cultures. Upon a relational view one's identity is tied to public roles that are continuously renegotiated as a social arrangement within a culture.

Who Is a Person: Demarcation by Competence or by Community?

The thorny question about *what* a person is, is closely intertwined with the question *who* can be counted as persons. Is it sufficient to understand the human person on the basis of skills, be it individual or communicative competencies? Or is one a person by being part of a human society? Such questions arise in bioethical discussions about abortion and euthanasia as well as in public discussions of the treatment of severely handicapped and senile persons (Mahowald 1995; Wildfeuer 1998). Should we ascribe personhood to the fertilized egg (the classical Catholic position)? Or should we ascribe personhood only to evolved human (or non-human) beings who are capable of knowing, willing and feeling, and who definitely possess the ability of making deliberations?

Intricate ethical questions like these have stretched and challenged our common-sense notions of being a person. Quite a few proposals advanced during the last decades have tried to overcome the contrast between individualistic and social conceptions of the human person. They combine emphasis on the individual competence of a person with awareness of the embodiment of human persons in wider human communities. Tristam Engelhart, Jr has proposed an influential distinction between 'persons in the strict sense', who are the individual bearers of rights and duties, and 'persons in the social sense', who are members of human societies and should be treated as persons even when actually lacking the characteristics of rationality and moral subjectivity. Examples of the latter would be infants or senile members of the human race (Engelhardt 1986). While this definition still has as its focal point the individualist tradition, it also encompasses human society as an extension of individualistic personhood.

Others see social interdependence not only as context of personhood but as constitutive for personhood. Persons are always participating in a collective history and are thus situated in concrete social and cultural structures: 'Persons come after and before other persons' (Baier 1985, 85). It is within the community of persons that the irreplaceable status of unique persons is discovered. Since persons are always situated, intersubjectivity precedes subjectivity.

Toward a Bio-Cultural Paradigm

Now, if the concept of human personhood is strongly embedded in moral discourse, one might infer that it is *not* a scientific concept and that we should not expect much from an exchange between science and theology on this issue (Kirschenmann 1999). In fact, among the natural sciences there is no discipline pertaining to the human person as such.

When the European Society for the Study of Science and Theology (ESSSAT) organized its seventh European conference in Durham in 1998, the topic of 'The Human Person in Science and Theology' was nonetheless chosen quite deliberately. The science–theology dialogue is no longer confined to discussions on physics, cosmology, and evolutionary biology. Psychology and the social sciences are becoming major players in the field as well, and thereby also cultural issues such as personhood. This recent development probably reflects the increasing awareness of the issue of complexity in the sciences as well as a new emphasis on the role of theology and philosophy in mediating between the sciences and the wider cultural arena.

The understanding of the human person, however, is also relevant for the sciences. After all, human persons do the science as well as interpret the results of science. Personal commitments and cultural matrices play a heuristic role in the construction and interpretation of scientific theories; it may even influence the evaluation of competing theories, at least in the more speculative domains of science. Moreover, the idea of personhood, though not scientific in itself, points to an important subject matter for scientific investigation. For instance, the neurosciences explore causal processes behind human consciousness, including the neural structures and circuits that are involved in the sense of 'being a self'. Even if a biological neuroscience of personal identity is currently (perhaps for ever) out of reach, features like experiential feelings of red, green, hard, soft, pleasure and pain (*qualia*) are already major objects of research. Also, the construction and development of higher-order functions of the human person like memory, self-reflection and second-order volitions has become a favorite object of study (Edelman 1992; Gazzaniga 1992).

Within the neurosciences there are competing research programs for explaining immediate experiences of sensation as well as experiences of personal identity (or lack of identity). Some assume that it is in principle possible to explain mental qualities on the basis of the biology of mammalian brains alone; such programs take an epiphenomenalist view of the human mind and could be considered as reductionist. Other groups seek to develop systems with artificial intelligence (AI) which would display some of the mental operations typical of human persons. If all relevant requirements for the emergence of a well-functioning mind could be identified, intelligent and feeling agents could be artificially produced. At least, that is the assumption of the so-called strong AI-program.

Distinct from both *physicalist reductionism* and *computational functionalism*, is a third paradigm, explored in the present volume. The majority of contributors to the present volume argue that the emergence and stabilization of the 'human person' requires a co-evolution of brain and culture, that is, of the formation and functionality of the *human body*, including the human brain, and of the construction, maintenance and development of *human societies* in which the mental capacities of human persons are exercised. We might call this view the *bio-cultural* paradigm. In the present book the reader will thus find a strong emphasis on the covalence of nature and nurture in the formation and development of human personhood. In consequence, the human person is not to be seen as merely a psychological phenomenon, putatively to be biologically explained. Rather, the human person emerges as a result of the *interference* between the biological roots of human personhood and the cultural nexus of which any human person is part.

As above indicated there has been an overall trend from individualistic towards relational conceptions of the human person in twentieth-century philosophy. This move will be reflected by a majority of contributors to the present volume. Already the so-called 'personalist' movement in German and French philosophy (e.g. Buber 1937; Mounier 1952) led to a breakthrough of a dialogical understanding of the human person. In this context, a holist anthropology was assumed according to which the human person is 'a body in the same degree that he is a spirit, wholly body and wholly spirit' (Mounier 1952, 3). What was missing in these discussions, however, was a more sustained reflection on the functions of the human body, in particular the human brain. Personalism saw the distinguishing mark of personal being in its capacity to *transcend* the natural conditions and conceived of the interhuman relationships (I–Thou) as fundamentally different from the relationship of human beings to non-human nature (I–it). As a consequence of this contrastive thought pattern, philosophies of the human person were divorced from scientific descriptions of human beings. Viewed with hindsight, the movement of dia-logical personalism can be interpreted as an attempt to block the influence of the natural sciences on our understanding of human persons. Such a divorce between the objective and the subjective, however, is untenable even on phenomenological grounds, since any human interrelation is always mediated by objective reality and social interactions (Pannenberg 1983, 173–8). Human persons not only have bodies, but are bodies, though bodies with remark-able emergent qualities. Human persons do not only live in private space, but also in natural and moral space.

Since existentialism and personalism have made such a lasting impact on modern theology, the appearance of this book marks a break with the bogus dichotomy between personal and empirical features of human existence. We believe it is pertinent to inquire how we may correlate theological and scientific descriptions of human beings while acknowledging built-in differences in perspective.

All authors grant a general naturalist perspective, according to which mental activities rely on the well-functioning human body. However, most authors agree that the human person cannot be exhaustively explained in the terms of the neurosciences, and perhaps cannot be understood at all as physical. They see the human person as co-constituted by a neuronal basis which affords psychological states of awareness, and by its participation in cultural worlds of meaning without which a personal identity could not be developed and maintained. Human persons are physically embodied agents displaying a variety of remarkable features.

Seven Features of Human Personhood

The modern Western concept of a human person is often assumed to have its roots more or less exclusively in Christian thought. This widely canvassed idea has been modified by scholars in Classical Studies (de Vogel 1963; Engberg-Pedersen 1990). Already in Stoic tradition we find the idea that human persons are naturally equipped with a common rational nature but are unique individuals (Cicero: *On Duties* I.107). Thus, Cicero uses the term 'person' (1) as a generic characterization, and (2) as a mark of an individuality which cannot easily be communicated to other persons. 'Person' both identifies *what* a human being is, namely, a rational being, and *who* this or that particular person is. Against this background, a 'person' was regarded (3) as a moral subject, accountable for his or her deeds.

This Stoic tradition can be said to be encapsulated in the later standard definition by the Christian philosopher Boethius (480– 524) who, in the treatise *On the Two Natures: Against Eutyches*, defined a person as 'the individual substance of a rational nature' (*naturae rationabilis individua substantia*). Human personhood is here defined as the *capacity* for rational discernment present in an *individual* human being. Interestingly, however, Boethius made this definition in the context of a christological argument for the unity of Jesus Christ. According to the Chalcedonian formula of 451, Christ has two natures, yet only a single *persona*. 'Without doubt the person of Christ must be one. For if he were two persons he could not be one; but to say that there are two Christs [a divine and a human] is nothing else than the madness of a precipitated mind' (*On the Two Natures* 4). Evidently, Boethius is concerned about maintaining the identity of Christ and wants to preclude a separation of God and humanity in the one unified person of Christ. In this usage, the term 'person' may also indicate (4) the self-identity or 'character' of a being, even if a person consists of different 'elements' and may develop through a longer period of time.

Boethius was nonetheless aware of the older concept of person as a theater mask through which sounds come forth (*per-sonare*). Whether the word 'person' actually has this Latin root as suggested by Boethius (*On the Two Natures* 3), or is imported from the Persian word *persu* (also meaning a mask), is not important here. Significant, however, is the way in which a social orientation seems to be implied in the more archaic notion of personhood. After all, a personal identity is one which becomes more or less manifest in communication. A further feature of personhood might thus be (5) the public roles entertained by an individual.

From all these features there is a route to the features of personhood highlighted in the Middle Ages and in modernity, namely (6) the superiority and (7) transcendence of the human person. According to Thomas Aquinas, the person is 'the most perfect of all in nature' and possesses, as such, an inherent 'dignity' (*Summa Theologiae* I.29.3). This concentration on the distinctiveness and excellence of the human person has influenced not only Protestant Kantianism, but has also, through Thomism, exercised a strong impact on twentieth-century Catholic thinking on the moral resources of personhood. Note, for example, how Pope Pius XII conceived of the human person in the thought pattern of a subject *transcending* objective conditions in a moral-religious act: 'the grandeur of the human act consists precisely in its transcending the very moment when it is performed, to commit the whole orientation of one's life, to lead it to adopt a stance in relation to the absolute' (quoted in Mahoney 1990, 221).

Even if one wants to emphasize the social constitution of personhood, this element of freedom or transcendence in relation to any given society seems to be non-negotiable. The society at large and local communities in particular may offer, or even (in the extreme) impose, a variety of roles onto the members of a society. However, the very fact that these roles must be affirmed or negated by human persons, and will be modified in this or in another direction during the role-performance of individuals, indicates that some notion of self-regulatory autonomy cannot be erased from the concept of personhood (Pannenberg 1983, 217f.). Only a polarity between social and subjective features seems to do justice to the scope of human existence.

Human and Divine Persons

So far we have listed seven features of the Western concept of personhood. There are, however, more specific resources in theological tradition which might prove valuable in a contemporary context. Christian tradition has thus developed a theology of the human being as created 'in the image and likeness of God' and has claimed that God exists in a perfection of personal life.

In their contributions to the emerging doctrine of the Trinity in the fourth century, the Cappadocian Fathers Basil the Great and the Gregories of Nyssa and of Nazianz, established new avenues for the concept of personhood. The divine substance (*ousia*) was claimed to be equally shared by the divine 'persons', the Father, the Son and the Holy Spirit. However, this divine substance does not exist *in abstracto*, but is only real within the triune relationship between the three persons. 'Person' is therefore no longer an adjunct to God's being, but is constitutive for the being of God. God's being (Gr. *hypostasis*) coincides with God's personhood (Gr. *prosopon* = Lat. *persona*).

This Nicene solution was revolutionary in so far as it implied that divine substance only exists in the form of relations and communications. As expressed in an influential study by the Orthodox theologian John D. Zizioulas: 'The being of God is a relational being: without the concept of communion it would not be possible to speak of the being of God' (1997, 17). The very concept of the divine persons was even defined as existing in relations. The Father is only Father in relation to the Son, the Son only Son in relation to the Father, etc. Only in the event of mutual self-giving and coinherence (*perichoresis*) does God exist as God. This understanding of the community of the divine persons may be said to articulate the biblical saying that God *is* love (1 John 4:16).

This early anticipation of a relational idea of personhood is indeed remarkable, though it could be argued that the inter-relations of the divine persons are still thought to be internal to the divine life, and not related to the created beings. From the trinitarian theology of personhood, Zizioulas nonetheless infers both a historical hypothesis and a comprehensive ontology of personhood. Zizioulas claims that our concept of personhood is 'purely a product of patristic thought' (1997, 27), a hypothesis which can hardly be considered historically correct. Further-more, he derives a whole ontology on the basis of the trinitarian relations. Because God – being a communion of persons – is free, God is above fate and can create the world out of God's own will, *ex nihilo*; because God the creator is a communion of persons, so are human beings persons freed from defining themselves on the basis of their bodily conditions and free to relate themselves to the larger community of the universal church; because God is a communion of persons, God can invite other persons into sharing God's life, as in the Orthodox concept of divinization. This highly suggestive picture conveys important insights and has attracted both Catholic and Protestant writers (LaCugna 1993, 243–328; Volf 1998, 73–126). The question remains, however, whether it is possible to deduce a comprehensive ontology from the Trinity, and whether theologians of today should argue for such a direct derivation of the human concept of personhood from the trinitarian concept of the personhood of God.

At least we should be very attentive to some of the differences between the trinitarian and the anthropological concepts of personhood. The Catholic church historian Basil Studer makes this point without reserve: 'If one is trying to compare the personal fellowship and personal development of human beings in some fashion with the divine life of the Father, Son and Spirit, one is best advised not to introduce this [trinitarian] concept of person into the equation' (1982, 177, quoted in Volf 1998, 199). For all, the very attempt to derive a theological understanding of the *human* person from the doctrine of the Trinity appears to go far beyond the intention of the Nicene Creed. The Cappadocian Fathers affirmed the apophatic rule that the inner divine relations are beyond human comprehension. On this ground, Orthodox theologians have criticized the more recent attempts of using the trinitarian concept of personhood as a general ontological model (Panagopoulos 1993). Positive resemblances and suggestive proposals should not make us blind to remaining differences.

The discussions in the present volume focus more on the anthropological tradition within Jewish and Christian thought. There may be a sufficient basis for developing a relational theology of the human person in the context of a renewed attention to the concept of humanity as created 'in the image and likeness of God' (Gen. 1:26f.). In the first creation story (Gen. 1:1—2:4a) there is an awareness that human beings are from the outset created as 'male and female', that is, within a field of relationships marked by partnership, co-operation, acceptance of otherness, and by the enjoyment of spiritual and bodily interaction. Also, the care for the offspring is included in the constitution of human beings. At least, the blessing is added to Adam and Eve as God's images: 'Be fruitful and multiply' (Gen. 1:28). So far, the features of the relationality of personhood seem to be well covered by the creation epos. To be a human means being embedded in a moral space of mutual attention, cooperation, and responsibility. In all this, there is a cointensification of spiritual and natural features. Just as marriage combines sex and love, so does work in the cultural realm include an interaction with the soil and dust, from which human beings were created in the first place. Likewise, some of the features related to the uniqueness and irreplaceability of individuals seems to be anticipated in the taboo against killing. Just after the renewal of God's blessing to Noah, it is said, 'Whoever sheds the blood of a human, by a human shall that person's blood be shed; for in his own image God made humankind' (Gen. 9:6). Killing other persons is murdering.

. We do not want, on behalf of Christian tradition, to claim any exclusiveness of these trinitarian and anthropological insights into personhood. But we think they show that the project of arguing for a bio-cultural paradigm is consonant with Christian tradition. A theological concept of personhood articulates both the sense in which human role-modeling transcends the role stereotypes of others as well as the feeling of a human resonance with the nature in us and outside us, and with the social realm in which we are incorporated. According to Christian assumptions, God demonstrates a specific personal 'character', an identity which elicits and embraces the personhood of others.

Contents of this Volume

In the present volume, the notion of 'the human person' will be discussed in an multidisciplinary perspective ranging from physiology, neuroscience and psychology to anthropology, philosophy and theology. The bio-cultural paradigm demands such a high degree of interdisciplinary cooperation, and we hope to demonstrate that the role of theology in understanding ourselves will not be decreased but rather increased if we see ourselves as biologically rooted, yet culturally embodied beings.

Philosopher **Mary Midgley** (Newcastle on Tyne, UK) argues that the 'problem of free will' is largely an artefact of Cartesian dualism. The idea that thought is ineffectual is not compatible with any real belief in our evolutionary continuity with the rest of nature; furthermore, epiphenomenalism rests on the fallacious assumption that there exists a complete 'physical' explanation of everything. According to Midgley, we need many maps to explore the same complex world, and we should look for a larger set of partial explanations rather than for one explanatory scheme.

The need for a variety of perspectives is also emphasized by psychologist and theologian **Fraser Watts** (Cambridge, UK). Both human emotion and religious experience illustrate the way in which biological and social aspects of personal life are intertwined.

As a discipline, psychology is bound to hold together the physical and the social factors. While Watts does not believe that the case for a non-reductive physicalism is yet settled, he opts (like Midgley) for a many-maps approach and refrains from general claims on causal primacy.

In the last decade the so-called gene myth has prevailed. Paediatrician **Hugo Lagercrantz** (Stockholm, Sweden) argues that the idea of a genetic determinism is a modern version of the old doctrine of preformation, which is not tenable. Even though a causal influence from genetic constitution to behavior should not be doubted, the development of the embryo shows that genetic determinism is not well warranted as a scientific hypothesis. The complexity and plasticity of the brain encourages us to believe that there is substantial room for exercising a free will in shaping our social and cultural environments.

Theologian **Philip Hefner** (Chicago, USA) also points out that the human person is a product of an evolution that is both biological and cultural. To be a person is not fully contained in our physical conditions, but also requires the marshaling of behavior in response to the cultural environment. In critical discussion with Paul Tillich and Wolfhart Pannenberg, Hefner regards the human person as grounded in a network of relationships between God, world, and Thou. In Hefner's interpretation, the human person is called to become an *imago dei*, that is, a portrayal of God's presence in the world.

Theologian **Michael Welker's** (Heidelberg, Germany) essay encapsulates many of the perspectives on human personhood covered in this volume. Taking his point of departure in the pre-modern concept of personhood as a mask, Welker questions the modern ideal of the 'agonal self' which constantly needs to strive for a personal consistency in a process of withdrawal from society and sensual nature. The ideal of the person behind the mask is no longer sustainable and Welker opts for a renewed communication between the subject behind the mask and the public self in front of the mask.

Philosopher of religion **Dennis Bielfeldt** (Brookings, USA) traces the history of the concept of supervenience and introduces the varieties of supervenience theories in current analytical philosophy of mind. Bielfeldt argues that there seems to be no room for a causal efficacy of the mental within the reigning philosophical paradigm of supervenience. The use of supervenience in recent science–theology dialogue nonetheless often assumes exactly this possibility. The question is whether a Christian theology can be developed on the premise of a causally closed physical universe or whether it is inescapably committed to an ontological dualism between God and world.

Theologian **Niels Henrik Gregersen** (Aarhus, Denmark) points out that there exist two versions of brain–mind supervenience in the current philosophy of mind. While Jaegwon Kim's physicalist supervenience believes in microdetermination of the mental from the brain, Donald Davidson's holist version of supervenience allows for an efficacy of the mental, because mental properties are relational and not intrinsic to the brain. The eucharistic experience of God's transformation of human minds by way of external words and signs is at variance with the first version, but is structurally conformal with the latter version of supervenience.

In a similar vein, psychologist **John Teske** (Elizabethtown, USA) contends that a variety of mental properties, including those of religion and spirituality, cannot be understood on the basis of the brain alone, but include a reference to culture. Building on John Searle's concept of institutional facts, Teske argues that mental life presupposes not only physical space, but also the semantic space offered by social institutions. The social interdependence of spiritual lives shows the importance of narratives and religious communities for the emergence and development of ourselves as human persons.

References

BAIER, ANETTE. 1985. *Postures of the Mind: Essays on Mind and Morals*, London: Methuen.

BUBER, MARTIN. [1923] 1937. *I & Thou*, Edinburgh: T&T Clark.

EDELMAN, GERALD M. 1992. *Bright Air, Brilliant Fire: On the Matter of the Mind*, New York: BasicBooks.

ENGBERG-PEDERSEN, TROELS. 1990. 'Stoic Philosophy and the Concept of Person', in C. Gill (ed.), *The Person and the Human Mind*, Oxford: Oxford University Press.

ENGELHARDT, H. T. 1986. *The Foundations of Bio-Ethics*, Oxford: Oxford University Press.

GAZZANIGA, MICHAEL S. 1992. *Nature's Mind: The Biological Roots of Thinking, Sexuality, Language and Intelligence*, New York: BasicBooks.

KIRSCHENMANN, PETER. 1999. 'The Elusive Nature of Persons', in *Studies in Science and Theology*, vol. 7, Aarhus: Aarhus University (forthcoming).

LACUGNA, CATHERINE MOWRY. [1991] 1993. *God for Us. The Trinity and Christian Life*, Harper: San Francisco.

MAHONEY, JOHN. [1987] 1990. *The Making of Moral Theology: A Study of the Roman Catholic Tradition*, Oxford: Clarendon Press.

MAHOWALD, MARY B. 1995. 'Person', *Encyclopedia of Bioethics*, rev. edn, New York: Simon & Shuster, 1934–41, vol. 4.

MOUNIER, E. [1946] 1952. *Personalism*, London: Routledge & Kegan Paul.

PANAGOPOULOS, JOHANNES. 1993. 'Ontologie oder Theologie der Person? Die Relevanz der patristischen Trinitätslehre für das Verständnis der menschlichen Person', *Kerygma und Dogma 39*, 2–30.

PANNENBERG, WOLFHART. 1983. *Anthropologie in theologischer Perspektive*, Göttingen: Vandenhoeck & Ruprecht.

RUDMAN, STANLEY. 1997. *Concepts of Person and Christian Ethics*, Cambridge: Cambridge University Press.

SCHRAG, CALVIN O. 1997. *The Self After Post-Modernity*, New Haven: Yale University Press.

STUDER, BASIL. 1982. 'Der Person-Begriff in der frühen kirchenamtlichen Trinitätslehre', *Theologie und Philosophie* 57, 161–77.

DE VOGEL, CHRISTINA. 1963. 'The Concept of Personality in Greek and Christian Thought', *Studies in Philosophy and the History of Philosophy* 2, 20–60.

VOLF, MIROSLAV. 1998. *After Our Likeness: The Church as the Image of the Trinity*, Grand Rapids/Cambridge: William B. Eerdmans.

WILDFEUER, ARMIN G. 1998. 'Person. Philosophisch', *Lexicon der Bioethik*, Gütersloh: Gütersloher Verlagshaus, vol. 3, 5–9.

ZIZIOULAS, JOHN D. [1985] 1997. *Being as Communion: Studies in Personhood and the Church*, Crestwood: St Vladimir's Seminary Press.

PART I:
TOWARDS A BIO-CULTURAL
PARADIGM OF PERSONHOOD

2

Consciousness, Fatalism and Science

MARY MIDGLEY

Dualistic Difficulties

I want to make a large and simple point. Science does not require us to accept fatalism.

The idea that it does is very common today, though theorists disguise it somewhat by using the word determinism rather than actually saying fatalism. This fatalistic bent largely accounts for the current fear of science. Fatalism itself is obviously not science at all. It is bad metaphysics which got entangled with science because the metaphysical climate that fostered modern science made it so hard to allow a proper role for consciousness as well as for matter. That metaphysic was, of course, Descartes' dualism – the radical separation of mind from body.

This dualism is really a very extraordinary view. If we were studying a Chinese vase, we would distinguish many different aspects of it such as its shape, its size, its colour, its history and its function. But we would not be likely to say that these aspects were themselves separate existing objects – objects so alien to one another that it was mysterious how they could interact at all.

But when we consider those two aspects of a human being which we now call Mind and Body, our current tradition does make us talk in this strange way. The radical split which Descartes established between these two aspects still divides our thought and our world. In many ways it has served us well, doing much to make the development of modern science possible. But, like other simple philosophical traffic-rules, it becomes counterproductive when we strain it beyond its proper function. And today its drawbacks are becoming painfully clear, above all on the topic which we call Free Will.

Free from What?

For a start, 'free will' is a bad name. The metaphor of *freedom* already gives a wrong picture. Freedom is a relation between two separate beings, an escaper and a potential controller. We can be free from a prison, or a master, or a tyrant, or a disease, because these are controlling entities distinct from *ourselves*. But we can't be controlled by our own bodies unless those bodies are, in just as full a sense, distinct from what we call 'ourselves'.

To talk of being controlled by our bodies is already to have accepted a special notion of ourselves, a notion which excludes those bodies. The term 'free will' originally meant simply freedom from outside compulsion, as in 'acting of one's own free will'. But it is now used, quite differently, to narrow our notion of our *self* to a peculiar thing called the Will by excluding our bodies from it. This usage changes our self-image, and also the image that we have of the outside world.

Descartes originally designed this notion of the separate self or mind to account for the fact that we have to talk in different ways when we are describing these two aspects of ourselves. Already in his day the two languages involved were diverging in a way that made trouble. So he split them apart by the extreme measure of calling them separate substances. Today, this strong, simple dualism is officially usually rejected. Yet it still persists and it is even being reinforced at present by computer imagery. Many people now find it perfectly natural to state – as a fact and not just as a metaphor – that mind is divided from body exactly as software is divided from hardware. ('The brain is a computer made of meat.') This approach gives dualism an even stronger grip. We need to be sure whether we really want this.

On Descartes' model, the physical world which includes our bodies is indeed one vast machine designed by God. Minds coexist outside it as conscious substances of a separate, parallel kind – extra programmers rather than software. But this story now seems very obscure. As time has gone on, minds have increasingly appeared as embarrassing extra entities and have gradually been dropped from the scientific picture. Thus, the image which has shaped our supposed modern problem of free will no longer shows human life as a drama where real people struggle against great external difficulties, but as one where they simply do not act independently at all. Only their bodies are left and these are mere passive cogs in a vast impersonal mechanism. *But this passivity is the situation of a paralysed person.* For anyone who is not actually paralysed, this radical fatalism presents no sort of usable way of life. If it had been taken literally and judged on its own merits, it would (therefore) probably not have been accepted. The reason why it caught on so easily is that it fits the powerful mass of rhetoric which we have inherited from earlier forms of fatalism. These forms were never meant to state scientific laws. They simply displayed a drama, which was recognised as a poetic image rather than literal fact, in which human beings felt themselves to be helpless victims of a remote or malignant Fate-figure. As Omar Khayyám put it:

'Tis all a chequer-board of nights and days
Where Destiny with men for pieces plays
Hither and thither moves and mates and slays
And one by one back in the closet lays.[1]

This imagery does not need a serious belief in a deity called Fate to support it. It simply provides a kind of universal excuse, a handy chance for everybody to take on the role of victim. Even declared atheists sometimes like to indulge in this fantasy and Renaissance astrology often invoked it. Thus, in John Webster's play *The Duchess of Malfi* a character (who has in fact been largely responsible for his own ruin) complains that

---

[1] Omar Khayyám's *Rubaiyat*, stanza xlix, translated by Edward Fitzgerald.

> We are merely the stars' tennis balls, struck and bandied
> Which way please them.[2]

We might have hoped that Descartes' effort to sterilise the physical world by calling it a *machine* would have discouraged this superstitious way of talking. Yet, only a century back, Thomas Hardy, who was an outspoken atheist, still ended his novel *Tess of the D'Urbervilles* with a kind of affectation of belief, writing that 'the President of the Immortals, in Aeschylean phrase, had ended his sport with Tess'. Still more surprisingly, scientists today who are nominally using the machine image as a weapon against superstition not only still employ this fatalistic rhetoric but have even intensified it, personifying parts of the cosmic machine itself as malignant fate-figures. Thus Richard Dawkins (1986, x and 3, cf. 215):

> We are survival machines – robot vehicles blindly programmed to preserve the selfish molecules known as genes.... We, and all other animals, are machines created by our genes. Like successful Chicago gangsters, our genes have survived, in some cases for millions of years, in a highly competitive world.... A predominant quality to be expected in a successful gene is ruthless selfishness ...

The message of Dawkins' book is that we are powerless elements in a machine which ignores our purposes and will deflect all our efforts – including, of course, our attempts to escape it – to serve its own alien ends. Though he evidently thinks this discovery important he does not explain how he thinks it ought to affect our life and conduct.

The critics of sociobiology have not paid much attention to this strangely impractical fatalism because in general they don't know how to answer it. They object, and with reason, to the sociobiological rhetoric. They would not use this language themselves. But in substance many of them, like other scientifically minded people today, think that they are committed to physicalistic fatalism. Though for practical purposes they wholeheartedly accept the assumption of 'free will' and confidently live their lives on that basis, they either suppose this assumption to be indefensible

[2] V.iv.52.

or are not sure how to defend it. They regard the 'problem of free will' as overwhelmingly difficult. And so it is, in the form in which it is now commonly posed. We need to rephrase it completely.

A Strange Story

I think the best way to start doing this may be to look more closely at the supposedly hard view to which many scientifically-minded people now seem committed. So far, they have accepted it because they saw that the other patterns available to them within the Cartesian paradigm were unworkable. But this last resort – this final Cartesian refuge – is no better than the rest. It is what makes our present difficulties look so crushing.

Let us have a look, then, at the steam-whistle theory of mind, usually called Epiphenomenalism. This is the theory that says that what happens in our consciousness does not affect the behaviour of our bodies. Our experience is just an 'epiphenomenon', that is, idle froth on the surface, a mere side effect of physical causes. Consciousness is thus an example of something surely quite unique in the universe, namely, of one-way causation. It is a result which does not itself cause anything further to happen.

I think this strange doctrine has been somewhat protected by its awkward and impressive name. That is why I am using a different one, a name drawn from T. H. Huxley, who invented the idea a century back. Huxley (1901, 240) wrote that consciousness, both in humans and animals,

> would appear to be related to the mechanism of their bodies simply as a collateral product of its working, and to be as completely without any power of modifying that working as the steam-whistle which accompanies the working of a locomotive is without influence on its machinery.

This view has since been backed by many influential theorists, notably B. F. Skinner. Colin Blakemore (1988, 269–70) has recently supported it, writing that

> The human brain is a machine which alone accounts for all our actions, our most private thoughts, our beliefs. It creates the state of consciousness and the sense of self. It makes the mind.... To choose a

spouse, a job, a religious creed – or even to choose to rob a bank, is the peak of a causal chain that runs back to the origin of life and down to the nature of atoms and molecules.... All our actions are the products of the activity of our brain ... We feel ourselves, usually, to be in control of our actions, but that feeling is itself a product of our brain, whose machinery has been designed, on the basis of its functional utility, by means of natural selection.

Blakemore does not explain how natural selection could 'design, on the basis of its functional utility' a faculty which does not in any way affect our behaviour, nor how it could then delude us into believing that there is such an effect. Evolutionarily speaking, both these moves seem impossible, and, even if they were possible, startlingly wasteful and pointless. (More generally, it is hard to see how any phenomenon *which had no effects* could enter into a causal process such as natural selection.) Francis Crick, too, leaves this evolutionary puzzle unexplained, though he has lately decided that he too has invented epiphenomenalism, calling it The Astonishing Hypothesis (1994).

Now I suggest that it is not helpful to repeat a doctrine that one can't actually believe in.

Shall we ask, then, what it would be like to be an actual believer in epiphenomenalism? Here is the scenario. Somebody (our old friend A) rings up a colleague, B, to ask for help. But B is a real epiphenomenalist – not the ordinary hypocritical kind. So he answers at once, 'No, I'm sorry, I can't do anything for you. You see, anything that I might try to do would involve conscious effort. And it is simply not possible for any conscious activity to have a real effect in the world. I can daydream about helping you. Indeed, I am doing so now. But that won't produce action. Consciousness is just an inert side effect of the real causal factors. You and I are both equally helpless and we must submit to the vast cosmic machine. What will be, will be.'

Determinism, as it is held today, is not usually supposed to involve such fatalism. But if determinism includes epiphenomenalism – as it is now widely thought to do – then it surely does require this fatalism. *The essential element in fatalism is the futility of effort – and effort (unlike desire) is necessarily something conscious.* The only reason why determinist writers don't notice this difficulty is that they usually think of it as applying to other people's activities, not to their own.

Even if they are uneasy about it, they think that their strange view is necessary because *they are still thinking of consciousness as a separate, supernatural entity – a dubious extra to be sliced off with Occam's razor – rather than as a normal activity, an emergent capacity acquired by social creatures during the regular course of evolution.* That is why they want to bracket this entity out of the causal sequence. But this excessive parsimony saws off the branch that it is sitting on. The attempt to treat conscious experience as ineffective radic-ally undermines itself. *All* our thought is predicated on the belief that we can put our decisions into practice, that we are not totally paralysed. A theory which ignores the difference between a norm-ally active person's thoughts about future action and those of a paralytic is not a realistic theory.

Effects on the Practice of Science

This is particularly obvious in the practice of science itself. Let us consider another character, C, who is trying to write a scientific article. C does not just sit still and think. After a time, his or her hand moves. C begins to make notes. And things do not end there. Still more aggressively, C now fetches a book, looks up a reference, and finds something that requires checking. C then telephones the lab to arrange to do an experiment, and later in the day actually does it.

Now we cannot treat C's conscious thoughts as mere effects of this behaviour (as B. F. Skinner did (1972)), because the time-order is wrong. The thoughts come first. They are its source, not its outcome. Nor can we treat those thoughts (as would more commonly be done today) simply as effects of activity in the brain. Of course that activity is needed if they are to occur. But his earlier thoughts, and a whole background of other people's thoughts, are needed too. And if we want *an explanation of C's actions*, the only place where we can find it is in those thoughts.

Suppose (for instance) that we ask why this researcher looked at this special page of this particular book rather than another, or proposed one particular experiment and did it in a particular way, the answer has to be in terms of its relevance to that ongoing train of thought. And *relevance simply is not a property of neurones.* It is a logical relation between ideas. In looking for this explanation, we shall not start to ask questions about C's brain-states unless his reasoning turns out to be crazy. And if that does happen, the brain-states will be used to explain the craziness, not the reasoning.

With the railway engine the situation is quite different. If we ask why this particular train started out at 6.15 for Cardiff rather than at 9 o'clock for Penzance, it is no use whatever to study the details of the steam whistle. The steam-whistle image was meant to suggest that conscious thought is just a clamorous and noticeable, but irrelevant, accompaniment of action. Sometimes indeed it can be so. People do 'get carried away', doing what they do not intend, and their action can then be unfree, driven, compulsive. But in cases such as that of scientific work – which is much more typical of ordinary action – conscious thought corresponds rather to the rail-way timetable and to the intentions of the people who composed it. It provides the only context in which we can explain those actions in the ordinary sense – that is, explain why they were done rather than something else. *This kind of explanation is not in competition with the kind which describes how the brain, and the railway engine, have to be in working order to make this kind of action possible. Both accounts are equally necessary, but for different purposes.* (Karl Popper argued this point very well in his essay 'Of Clocks and Clouds' (Popper 1972, 222–4), but he drew the moral that it called for dualism. As we have seen, this is a mistake.)

So the reason why we do not normally seek neuronal explanations for people's actions is not – as physicalists suggest – that neurology is still too incomplete. It is that those explanations lie in the wrong direction. They are simply not answers to the kind of questions that we usually need to ask in order to explain actions. They answer questions of a different kind. The fact that there are questions of different kinds may be troublesome but it is one that we have to take account of. We will come back to this troublesome feature of the world later.

Freedom and Responsibility

One factor which epiphenomenalism cannot possibly accommodate, but which is of pervading importance in real life, is, of course, responsibility. B. F. Skinner (1972) made great efforts to get rid of this concept entirely. Colin Blakemore, attempting the same feat recently, has suggested (1988, 269–70) that we ought not to draw any distinction between deliberate actions and reflexes:

> All our actions are products of the activity of our brains. It seems to me to make no sense (in scientific terms) to try to distinguish sharply between acts that result from conscious intention and those that are pure reflexes or that are caused by disease or damage to the brain.
>
> The sense of will is an invention of the brain. Like so much of what the brain does, the feeling of choice is a mental model – a plausible account of how we act, which tells us no more about how decisions are really taken in the brain than our perception of the world tells us about the computations involved in deriving it.

Now of course it is true that the distinction between responsible and irresponsible action is not a *sharp* one. But then no sensible person thinks it is. Our culture acknowledges many kinds and degrees of responsibility, many kinds of subtle excuses and mitigations to avoid the danger of unfair punishment – a danger which rightly concerns Blakemore, as it did Skinner.

But *punishment* affects only a tiny corner of the area involved. Blakemore is not talking only about how sharp this distinction is. He is asking whether there should be any distinction at all between meaningful, deliberate action and spasmodic movement caused by a reflex. But, as we have seen, this distinction is vital to the practice of science itself, including writings about consciousness. If a scientist were proved to have composed his article entirely by luck, merely by a series of muscular twitches as he sat at the keyboard without ever thinking the thoughts that seem to be expressed in it, he would not be considered responsible for that article and he would get no credit for it.

Demythologising the Selfish Brain

The idea that, right across this range, everybody is really as non-responsible as people driven by disease or by reflex is not workable, especially – as I mentioned earlier – from the angle of evolution. Blakemore credits that potent and sinister planner 'the brain' with inventing the sense of will and the feeling of choice in order to mislead us. But this again is the language of traditional fatalism. We must surely ask: What had 'the brain' to gain from actively misleading us in this way? or – to speak more intelligibly – how could it be worth the whole organism's while to develop, at considerable circulatory cost, a misleading apparatus for consciousness whose only function is to make trouble by demanding plausible stories to keep it quiet?

People are driven to defend these wild positions because they assume that explanation must always follow the same form. They rightly do not want to interrupt the neurological story by inserting occasional bits of conscious thought into it. And they do not see how a parallel mental story can be anything other than a dangerous rival.

But the neurological story is always essentially incomplete because the brain is not the whole person. Nor (of course) is it a sinister inventor, a puppet-master who constructs the rest of the person as its helpless plaything. The brain is simply a part of us, a useful (though rather complicated) bit of meat packed inside our skulls. It does not make us think; we think with it, as we walk with our feet and digest with our internal organs. No doubt the neurological account of brain-processes is continuous in its own terms. But that process is also part of a wider process which has to be observed from other angles as well. A human being is, in fact, rather like a vast, ill-lit aquarium containing a busy population of fish and plants which we can only observe through a number of windows spaced out round its outer wall. Observers at the different windows need to co-operate rather than competing for sole dominion. The neurological window is important, but it cannot tell the whole story.

The fact that, when certain neurones come into play, their owner is asking an awkward question about chemistry could never become apparent from the neurological data alone. And even if those neurones could be identified they would still do nothing to *explain the thought*. That must always be done in its own terms. For instance, if a neurologist had had a chance to observe Pythagoras' brain fully just before he invented his theorem, that neurologist still could not have foreseen this theorem – unless, of course, the neurologist himself happened also to be a mathematician with gifts and information very close to Pythagoras' own. And in that case he would have invented it rather than foreseen it. The two stories follow different tracks and do not intersect, though they are both stories about the same person.

What gives constant trouble here is the picture of the neurones as forcing the thought. They no more force it than a plant's genes force the plant to grow. There is no resistance. The brain supplies part of the means of thought and the genes supply part of the means for the plant's growth – a part that has, incidentally, been considerably exaggerated during recent decades.[3] Political metaphors of compulsion and exploitation are mere anthropomorphic fantasies here. It is the agent as a whole that acts. And that agent acts freely in so far as he or she is free from various forms of what Spinoza called Human Bondage – for instance, paranoia, prejudice, self-deception, ignorance, sloth, cowardice and other genuine faults. These are the kind of defects that threaten human freedom – not the normal influence of the bodies through which we live and act.

Dualism and Metaphysical Warfare

To sum up, then, so far: Epiphenomenalism is not compatible with the central structure of concepts which makes human thought and action, including science, possible. B's excuse is not an incomplete bit of science, containing some useful half-truth. It is ordinary humbug. It is what Sartre called 'bad faith'. It rests on no facts, scientific or otherwise, merely on epiphenomenalist doctrine. And

---

[3] On the melodramatic exaggeration of the genes' actual role in development which has accompanied this personification see *Refiguring Life* by Evelyn Fox-Keller (1995), especially the quotation on p. 27.

that doctrine is not itself a fact. It is a piece of metaphysics, part of the conceptual map on which we have been organising our ideas. In fact, it is an extension of a piece of metaphysics which is visibly reaching the end of its useful life in all kinds of areas, namely Descartes' dualism, the crude, simple plan of splitting human beings into two quite separate parts, mind and body.

Descartes meant that dualism to act as a traffic-regulation, separating the physical sciences which deal with objects from the humanities, which deal with subjects. Above all, he meant it as a protective railing to save the tender shoots of physics from being eaten by alien organisms such as theology. But all that was a long time ago. Today, the mighty tree of physics does not need these protective railings. In fact, physics itself has recently broken through them by bringing into quantum mechanics questions about observers. These questions are generally understood as questions about subjects, despite attempts to confine them to the recording apparatus.

Meanwhile, the social sciences, which have grown up all along that awkward Cartesian frontier, have long been in trouble trying to make sense of a customs barrier which splits them down the middle. This unrealistic division has also gravely distorted medicine, especially psychiatry. And it has distorted our understanding of evolution, where it has been used to disconnect the idea of mind, not just from the body, but from all the rest of evolved nature. In all these contexts, we need to understand that *we are not forced to choose between two different kinds of units, mind and body. The unit is the whole person.*

The Return of the Subject

Because of these difficulties, the behaviourist attempt to build a world consisting only of objects has clearly broken down. Questions which involve people and animals as subjects as well as objects are arising all over the sciences as well as in philosophy. This is why the 'problem of consciousness' has now become urgent. There is not just one such problem but a whole range of conceptual difficulties, suppressed throughout the behaviourist epoch but now demanding our notice. It is, however, still very hard to see how to deal with them. Today's scientists have been sternly trained to think that all rational thought has to follow a single pattern, namely, the pattern designed for the study of objects. So they still tend to force subjects onto that same Procrustean bed.

For example – if we ask how it is that C's thoughts can produce acts appropriate to them (such as checking a particular reference and setting up a particular experiment) we are likely to feel that we ought to look for universal causal laws governing such processes, laws modelled perhaps on the laws of physics.[4] But we cannot find that kind of law here, because *appropriateness* simply is not a concept of physics. The laws of a particular science only operate within it, not between it and its conceptual neighbours, where wider, structural considerations have to be used. That is why theorists concluded that the link between thought and the action that embodies it is unreal and must simply be denied.

That link, however, is by far the best-attested causal connection in our whole experience. Though it admits of occasional exceptions, most of the time our lives continually verify it. Indeed it may well be the model on which we originally conceive all other causal connection. Yet for half a century scientists have denied that link with a fervour and conviction that will surely provide future sociologists with a topic for investigation. During this time, people who were unhappy about losing this vital way of explaining human behaviour have been told to have faith that the strict causal laws to replace it would one day be provided – by neurology.

But why pick on neurology? Innumerable kinds of causes and conditions are necessary to bring about C's action – social causes, educational causes, economic, political, climatic, nutritional, genetic, medical causes, besides the subjective and neural angles that we have noticed. Each of these sets of causes may partially explain the action. But none of them invalidates the others; there is room for them all. The question 'which of them counts as *the*

---

[4] This is the solution proposed by David Chalmers in his influential article (1995).

explanation' in a given case depends entirely on our interests, on what we want to find out.

The current language of determinism, however, allows specialists in any of these topics to feel that they alone possess the genuine explanation – others being merely secondary. Thus we get the odd spectacle of many competing hyphenated determinisms – genetic determinism, economic determinism, neurological determinism and so forth. Each discipline apparently claims to have found the engine which really runs all the other causes, and therefore runs the train. This is another point on which the notion of *determinism* needs to be clarified.

Escape Routes

So, what is to be done? Centrally, I think, we must really get it into our heads that there are many non-competing sorts of explanation. Explanations vary because they are answers to questions and there are many kinds of question that human beings can want to ask. Like the Chinese vase that I mentioned at the start, all complex topics need to be looked at from many angles. And among those complex topics human behaviour is surely one of the most complex.

Instead (then) of the steam whistle, let us consider it for a moment as the vast, rather ill-lit aquarium that I mentioned earlier. There are a number of windows through which we can look into this aquarium, but there is no comprehensive view of it from above. Fish, and other more mysterious creatures, swim in and out among the rocks and weeds. When we lose sight of them at the window belonging to a particular science they sometimes come into view at a neighbouring one. Sometimes, however, they swim right into the foliage and can only be glimpsed – if at all – from the far side, where we carry on our subjective life. Thus, when our friend C is thinking seriously and acting on those thoughts, we can no longer follow what he or she is doing through the peephole of neurology. The fish have moved out of its reach. We must shift to the quite different standpoint of awareness, through which we easily trace the conceptual connections of thought and action. Of course we take up this position quite unthinkingly because we are using that standpoint all the time. Without it, our lives would fall to pieces. Yet it, too, is only one of the complementary positions that we constantly need.

The Many-Maps Model

This diversity of questions is really the main topic of this article. Accepting it is not a licence for anarchy and confusion. Rational thought uses many patterns, which can be connected intelligibly in many other ways besides trying to reduce them to uniformity. The reductive pattern that was devised in the seventeenth century to connect the various physical sciences has been extremely successful there, but experience has shown that we cannot use it everywhere.

That reductive pattern tells us to order different ways of thinking in a hierarchy running down from the superficial to the fundamental, a linear sequence which will fill the whole logical space available for explanation. The more fundamental thought patterns at the bottom are then called 'hard', while the upper layers are 'soft'.

This rather mysterious tactile metaphor evidently expresses a value judgement. The upper or 'softer' layers, which include history and literature, are seen as relatively superficial, amateurish, non-serious, because they fall short of the ultimate explanation. Classed as folk psychology,[5] they are tolerated, if at all, only as makeshifts to be used when the real scientific account isn't available, or when it is too cumbersome to use. They are just stages on the way down to the only fully mature science, namely physics.

The metaphor of *levels*, which is often used to describe the relation between these various ways of thinking, may seem to endorse this one-dimensional pattern. But what sense does this sort of linear hierarchy make? It really is not clear at all how we could even begin to treat the various kinds of reasoning involved in non-scientific branches of thought such as history, logic, law, linguistics,

---

[5] I have discussed the meaning of this curious phrase in *The Ethical Primate*, pp. 33 and 48.

musicology, and indeed mathematics as stages on the way to any physical science, let alone physics.

I suggest, then, that we put this familiar linear pattern aside entirely for the moment and consider a quite different conceptual map drawn from the homeland of all maps, geography. We might call it the Many-Maps Model.

At the beginning of our atlases, we find a great many maps of the world. My atlas gives: World Physiography (Structure and Seismology), World Climatology (Mean Annual Precipitation, Climatic Fronts and Atmospheric Pressure), World Vegetation ... World Political, World Food, World Air Routes and a lot more. These maps all represent the world differently. But *there are not many worlds*. How do we relate these varying pictures?

We do not need to pick on one of them as fundamental. We don't need to find a single atomic structure belonging to that map and justify the other patterns by reducing them to it. Nor do we need to bring in physics, which has already done that atomising job for us in a way that is not relevant to the present problem. What we need is something different. We have to relate all these patterns in a way that shows the connection between them, shows why there is room for them all and why they are not contradicting each other – not rival pictures representing separate alternative worlds.

To do this, we always draw back to look at the larger context of thought within which the different sets of questions arise. *Explanation, in fact, works by widening the context, not by atomising the structure.* There is nothing irrational about this outward move. We see the different maps as answering different kinds of question, questions which arise from different angles. They are all questions about the same enormous world, which can rightly be described in all these different ways because it is much bigger than all of them. The sense of that wider background is what holds the maps together without any risk of anarchy. There is nothing irrational about the fact that there is logical space left between the various kinds of question because we do not claim – as the seventeenth-century theorists did – to have a supermap uniting all the maps in a single system. Though these claims were still made by some Marxists, they have been found to be ungrounded.

We relate our various maps by following the coastlines which appear on all of them, showing common patterns. These patterns refer us back to what we know of the wider context. For instance, political maps, especially maps of Africa and Australia, often show mysterious straight lines of a kind not found on other maps. (There are no straight lines in nature.) The only way to understand these mysterious straight lines is to relate them to the history of particular treaties and to the colonial system that produced them. But treaties are not things that can be explained in terms of physiography or vegetation or electrons. Nor can they be explained in terms of the neurones of the people who make them, any more than vice versa. Treaties can only be explained by talk about human history and human purposes. This talk cuts into the cosmic cake, so to speak, from a quite different angle.

Understanding the relation of history to physiography is not like relating two places on the same map. It involves relating two maps – two different ways of thinking – to one another. And this is what we have to do when we consider problems about the relation of consciousness to the physical sciences and, in general, to the rest of human life.

Accepting Discontinuity

This discontinuity between different viewpoints and different languages is really my main topic. It is not a gratuitous invention of philosophers, not something alien imported into science from the humanities. It is an unavoidable difficulty. Within the sciences themselves it often crops up at the borders between different scientific disciplines which think in different ways. But the central and most awkward discontinuity is indeed always the one that is bothering us now – the frontier between subject and object, between the world as we see it from the inner viewpoint and the world as we learn about it, more 'objectively', from report and cultural consensus. That is where the 'problem of free will' arises.

This is not just a rough place that will be smoothed over some day by academic conquest. These two ways of thinking will always remain distinct and continue to tell us different things about the world. They are distinct in rather the same sort of way as our sense of sight is distinct from our sense of touch. We cannot feel colours nor see hardness and softness directly. But this distinctness is not hostility. These are complementary contributions. We are used to using both together. We can combine them provided that we don't take sides between them, treating one or the other as infallible. We can relate our inner and outer lives intelligibly in the same sort of way in which we relate sight and touch – by placing both in the wider context of the life around us, to which they both constantly contribute.

For instance – we think of our scientist as being responsible for the article he writes, as being entitled to credit for it. The notion of responsibility that we use here is a moral notion, not a scientific one, but it is crucial for the practice of science. Such notions have been built up out of endless data, both objective and subjective, and are still constantly being reshaped by both kinds of considerations.

Of course our ideas about responsibility are never complete. We must continually be reshaping them. But despite their faults, this whole moral approach is not a provisional, amateur stop-gap that will one day be replaced by a scientific view. It asks the questions that are appropriate when we are dealing with the subject matter of human conduct, appropriate to a crucial interest for which its purely scientific investigation would simply not be helpful at all. Without moral notions of this kind, we could not begin to think about how to treat one another, and the notions that we have, despite their faults, have been shaped by hard experience over the centuries in order to avoid certain gross and pernicious errors. Skinner's idea of scrapping this whole heritage and substituting simple rules drawn from a single supposedly scientific angle was not realistic at all.

Complexity Is Not Surprising

In conclusion, you may ask: Am I perhaps exaggerating our troubles? Do we really need to invoke as surprising a parallel as that furnished by geography if we want to understand the relation between our inner and outer viewpoints on life? Is this parallel in order? I think it is. The reason why geographers need many kinds of map is that the world is a pretty complex thing. But then, we ourselves are surely rather complex things too. Indeed, geography and psychology have quite a lot in common. Both are groups of very diverse subjects rather than single sciences. There is nothing wrong with that diversity. Indeed, there is a great deal right about it because in both cases the situation requires it. People sometimes say that the human brain is the most complex item in the universe. This cannot actually be right because the whole person to whom that brain belongs is a much more complex item than the brain alone. Like the Chinese vase from which we started, this whole person has many aspects. And neither the person nor the vase can be understood without knowing a good deal about the society they belong to.

Now it is surely not surprising if our understanding of something as complex as this is necessarily partial, divided and incomplete? We ourselves are not pure, omniscient minds standing outside the universe and equipped to find its ultimate structure. We are evolved animals, working under difficulties from inside the system. We use a haphazard mix of faculties which are not fully unified, but which give us various different sorts of useful light. We had surely better try to use them realistically.

References

BLAKEMORE, COLIN. 1988. *The Mind Machine*, London: BBC Books.

CHALMERS, DAVID. 1995. 'Facing Up to the Problem of Consciousness', *Journal of Consciousness Studies* 2.3, 200–19.

CRICK, FRANCIS. 1994. *The Astonishing Hypothesis: The Scientists' Search for the Soul*, London: Simon & Schuster.

DAWKINS, RICHARD. 1986. *The Selfish Gene*, Oxford: Oxford University Press.

FOX-KELLER, EVELYN. 1995. *Refiguring Life: Metaphors of Twentieth-Century Biology*, New York: Columbia University Press.

HUXLEY, T. H. 1901. *Methods and Results,* New York: Appleton & Co.

MIDGLEY, MARY. 1994. *The Ethical Primate,* London: Routledge.

POPPER, KARL. 1972. *Objective Knowledge: An Evolutionary Approach,* Oxford: Clarendon Press.

SKINNER, B. F. 1972. *Beyond Freedom and Dignity,* London: Jonathan Cape.

3

The Multifaceted Nature of Human Personhood: Psychological and Theological Perspectives

FRASER WATTS

In this chapter I intend to bring psychological and religious perspectives on the person into dialogue. The main theme will be the need, from both perspectives, to have a broad concept of the person that includes both biological and social aspects. I will begin by showing how the study of human emotions within psychology illustrates the importance of holding together biological and social aspects of being human. I will then extend this theme to the scientific study of religious experience, before considering more explicitly theological perspectives on personhood.

Emotions

Human emotions illustrate very well the way in which biological and social aspects of our personal life are intertwined. Emotions undoubtedly have both biological and social aspects, and any attempt to deny either one leads to a very impoverished account of them.

Our physical being is critically involved in emotional reactions; in fact it is doubtful whether there could be anything that could properly be called an emotion that did not have a physiological substrate. It is also possible to discern the evolutionary value of emotions. There is a growing consensus that the functional value of emotions is to enable us to redirect our plans and goal orientation with great rapidity (e.g. Oatley 1992). For example, faced with a threat of some kind, our anxiety enables us to redirect our energies to cope with it. Also, emotions are not unique to humans but are found in the animal kingdom. However, there is a depth of interiority in human emotions that makes them radically different from animal ones. There have been those who have tried to argue that the biological aspects of emotions are primary. For example, William James tried to argue that emotional feelings are just the way in which we become conscious of the bodily changes which are the core of emotional reactions, though this is a view which has proved too simplistic (see Oatley and Jenkins 1996).

Emotions are socially embedded too. They nearly always occur in an interactional context, and represent a response to another person. There are important social rules that influence how we interpret the situations that give rise to emotions. Though there are fundamental emotions such as fear and anger that occur with only minor variations in most cultures, there are many more subtle emotions which depend heavily on the social and cultural context. Emotions like guilt, embarrassment and resentment depend on the moral order (e.g. Harré 1986). Moreover, emotions have powerful social effects; our relationships are heavily dependent on our emotional response to those with whom we interact. There is no place for either biological or social imperialism about emotions.

Emotions are a context in which the opposition between social and biological aspects of personhood has been particularly marked, but they have also been the focus of another duality between emotion itself and human rationality. Western culture has tended to adopt what many would call the 'myth of the passions', in which the noble aspect of being human is presumed to be rationality, and the passions are regarded as the irrational side of us, and liable to lead us astray. There is a growing consensus among philosophers who have emphasised the rationality of emotions (e.g. Solomon 1993; De Sousa 1987), and psychologists who have emphasised their cognitive aspects (e.g. Williams *et al.* 1997) that this view is radically mistaken. Our emotions arise from a cognitive interpretation of the world, and enable us to adapt appropriately to it. In that sense, our emotions are intertwined with, and indispensable to, our rationality.

Unfortunately, the Christian tradition in the modern period has sometimes adopted this myth of the passions, and has shared the prevailing view of the passions as dangerous (Watts 1997). This is something that urgently needs to be reconsidered. In fact, there is much in the Christian tradition that can enable us to take a fresh and more positive view of the value of emotions. There is no useful prayer life without feeling; our knowledge of God is a knowledge of the heart, not merely of the head; the religious life involves an education of our emotional life in which virtuous and sinful forms of emotions are distinguished, and so on.

The concept of 'passions' was actually only half of the theory of what we would now call emotions (see Dixon 1999). In the early modern period, the era in which Christian thinkers particularly reflected on how the passions could lead us astray, theologians such as Jonathan Edwards also considered the 'affections', the term they used when considering the positive role in the Christian life of what we would now call 'emotions'. Though the term 'emotion' goes back a long way, it only became the dominant concept in the latter part of the nineteenth century with a general move towards a more explicitly secular view of human beings. Both passions and affections were considered in relation to the soul, and against a backdrop of a moral and religious world view. The concept of emotions, as it has developed over the last 150 to 200 years, was intended to be a more neutral and, in that sense, secular concept.

With the shift from the concept of passion to that of emotion went a similar shift from the concept of soul to the more secular concept of mind (Reed 1997). Psychology has always been somewhat confused about what it is studying (mind, behaviour or whatever), but normally does not see itself as the science of the soul, though it is possible to reconstrue the soul as an emergent property of human beings, in a way that is compatible with a modern scientific view of the person (Watts 1998). In general, psychology has taken a naturalistic view of its subject matter, one that ignores the impact of the moral order in which human beings operate (though it may offer naturalistic theories to explain morality).

It is a moot point how successful the avowedly secular concept of emotion has been. It has already been noted that social psychologists of emotion such as Harré have seen the need to emphasise again the moral order in which emotions arise, and I think it can be argued that the attempt to construct a view of our emotional life that neglects the moral and spiritual context is proving to be inadequate. That is a reappraisal that theologians can welcome, of course, and they will have a particular contribution to make to the contemporary discussion of the basis of emotions in the moral world, and their significance in the context of human flourishing and salvation. More generally, the growing espousal of a view of emotions that is both biological and social has also made it possible to recover some of the richness of the earlier Christian view of the passions and affections.

A Multifaceted Approach to Religious Experience

I want now to explore the significance of this broad approach to human functioning for religious experience. In keeping with what I have said so far, I want to emphasise the importance of a multifaceted approach to religious experience. This may sound trite, but in fact it is rather controversial, and many of those who are considering religious experience at the present time think *either* that the brain processes underpinning it are fundamental and that everything else is secondary, *or* that social-cultural aspects are fundamental and that everything is secondary to that. I disagree with both of those positions.

Of course, the brain is involved in religious experience, as it is in experience of every kind. How could it not be? Also, there is no conceivable reason why religious people should resist that obvious point, unless they fear that once they have admitted the involvement of the brain at all, there will be no stopping point before full biological reductionism.

One of the best known of current approaches to the neural basis of religious experience is that it arises from processes identical to, or at least similar to, those involved in temporal lobe epilepsy. However, the data on which this theory is based are methodologically weak, and the theory goes far beyond the data (see Jeeves 1997, ch. 4 for a critique). The theory that religious experience has the same neural substrate as epilepsy is based on two empirical claims, one that religious and epileptic experiences are phenomenologically similar, the other that people with temporal lobe epilepsy are particularly prone to religious experiences. Both empirical claims are in fact highly suspect. I am glad that the 'epilepsy' theory of religious experience is so weakly supported. Though I am completely happy with the investigation of the neural basis of religious experience, I would find the conclusion that it was based on a malfunctioning of the human brain uncongenial.

A more promising, though somewhat speculative, theory is that of d'Aquili and Newberg (1998) who have tried to identify which of the general-purpose 'cognitive operators' of the brain have a particular role in religious experience. They suggest that particularly important are the 'holistic operator' which underpins the religious sense of unity, and the 'causal operator' which underpins the belief in providence. Though I don't think this theory will survive unrevised, it seems to be the right kind of theory. Key points are (*a*) that it doesn't postulate some completely separate neural basis of religious experience, (*b*) that it doesn't link religious experience to malfunctioning of the brain, and (*c*) that it is not necessarily reductionist. The theory can be taken simply as pointing to the kind of neural processes which are *involved* in religious experience; it need not be taken as saying that religious experience is 'nothing more than' the functioning of particular neural processes.

There are also those who have emphasised the private and subjective aspect of religious experience, notably William James in his still powerful masterpiece *The Varieties of Religious Experience* (1960), first published at the turn of the century. James is admirably aware of the minefields in this area and avoids many of them. He is good, for example, on what he calls 'medical materialism', the attempt to undermine the truth claims of particular beliefs or experiences by pointing to the physical processes that underlie them (pp. 34 ff.). James is also aware of the ambiguity of what one ought to mean by 'religious'. He sees that there is a case for taking a broad view of it to include whatever is 'most primal and enveloping and deeply true' (p. 53). However, he also sees that such a broad definition is 'inconvenient', as he puts it; and he narrows his attention to the 'feelings, acts and experiences of individual men in their solitude, so far as they apprehend themselves to stand in relation to whatever they consider the divine' (p. 50).

However, James has his limitations. One of his blind spots is his failure to give proper consideration to the social and cultural aspects of religious experience. This is something for which he was heavily criticized early on by von Hugel (1923), and for which he has continued to be criticized. His bias is apparent in his very definition of religious experience as what individual men experience 'in their solitude'. Because he hopes to go some way to validating religion on the basis of a scientific study of religious experience, he has a strong wish to regard religious *experience* as primary, and doctrines and religious practices as secondary.

There has recently been a chorus of criticism of this Jamesian minimisation of the social aspects of religious experience, from a philosophical point of view by Katz (1978) and Proudfoot (1985), and from a more theological point of view by Lash (1988). Of course, up to a point, the critics are right. Social and cultural factors are enormously important in shaping all experience, including religious experience. It is easy to point to the qualitative differences between the religious experiences of different cultures as support for this. However, I believe that these criticisms of James are often overstated (see Watts 1997), and the implausible suggestion is made that the social is primary and the individual is secondary. That is going too far. To repeat, I am opposed to all claims of primacy as being implausible given the systemic nature of what it is to be human. We need to consider the biological, individual and social aspects of religious experience in a balanced way and to avoid giving primacy to any of them.

The Theology and Biology of Being Human

I have proposed a general approach to being a person that takes the biological and social aspects of personhood into account in a balanced way. I want now to see how this relates to theological concepts of personhood. First, let us consider how the current scientific emphasis on the biological aspects of human nature squares with the theological tradition.

At first blush there is a contrast of approaches here. Scientific and theological formulations of human nature often have a very different focus. Even where there is no clear incompatibility, their focus of interest shows very little overlap. One key difference concerns biology. Scientific approaches to human beings often emphasise biological aspects, whereas the theology of being human generally neglects biology. In contrast, moral aspects of being human are often emphasised in theological formulations, particularly as they bear on sin and salvation (e.g. Anderson 1982; Farley 1990).

Though there is an apparent contrast in the emphasis on physical aspects of human nature in science and theology, there is currently a move to minimize these differences (Brown 1998). The claim is that Christian theology and contemporary science are at one in emphasising the unity of the human person. It is held that both take an integrated view of body and brain on the one hand, and of mind, soul, personality and spirit on the other. This involves arguing that science is not as reductively physicalist as it seems, and that the Judeo-Christian tradition is not as dualist as is sometimes supposed.

Clearly, there is a point here. The Hebrew tradition is of an 'ensouled body', and does not take as dualist a view of soul as do many Greek thinkers in the Platonic tradition. Of major theologians, Aquinas, who took as Aristotelian a view of soul as anyone, is a good touchstone of the more holistic strand of Christian thinking about the person. All that can be readily admitted. However, it seems to me that it is easy to exaggerate the similarity of Christian theology and contemporary science about these things. Yes, Hebrew thought does generally assume an ensouled body (or a enspirited body), rather than a pre-existent soul that enters the body. Yes, it does on occasion even emphasise the continuity between our natural being and that of the animal kingdom. However, even in a passage such as Ecclesiastes 3:18–21 which incorporates that theme, we are in a thought world that is a long way removed from what would be assumed by modern science. 'The fate of man and beast is identical; one dies, the other too, and both have the self-same breath ... Who knows if the spirit of man mounts upward or if the spirit of the beast goes down to the earth?'

Yes, the Christian tradition, in the Apostle's Creed for example, does emphasise the resurrection of the body rather than the survival of a disembodied soul. In this it is more holistic than many people imagine. Yet, as far as I know, there is no classical theologian, not even Aquinas, who entirely dispenses with the survival of the soul in some form prior to the resurrection of the body. In the mainstream Christian tradition, there is certainly an emphasis on the resurrection of the body, but this complements a doctrine of the survival of the soul rather than being an alternative to it. Seen in this light, the Christian tradition is again a long way from what contemporary neuroscience could accept.

Contemporary neuroscience clearly espouses some form of 'physicalism', by which I mean the doctrine that we are essentially physical creatures in whom the complex functioning of our physical nature gives rise to whatever mental powers we have. One of the key issues for Christians is whether, and in what sense, it is possible to be a physicalist without being a reductionist. There are many people these days, both philosophers and theologians, saying that they are 'non-reductive physicalists' (Murphy 1998), and that the notion of 'supervenience 'makes this possible. The key question is whether it is actually possible to be a non-reductive physicalist. Despite the popularity of the position, it can be argued that it is internally incoherent to be a physicalist without also being a reductionist. Though non-reductive physicalism is an attractive position, I think the jury is out on whether it is tenable. Until the matter is resolved, it would be unwise to assume that non-reductive physicalism represents the salvation of Christian theology of the person.

The scientific tradition is actually more confused on these matters than attention to neuroscience alone would suggest. One of the intriguing things is that artificial intelligence (AI) and neuroscience have quite different background assumptions on mind–body questions. Many of the same scientists are involved in the two fields, though they are often not fully aware of the metaphysical gulf between them. Though neuroscience is explicitly physicalist, AI is explicitly not so, but is based on a 'functionalist' view of mind. The assumption of AI is that the human mind can be implemented in a variety of different contexts, not only in the human body, but also in computer hardware.

There is quite a fierce dispute going on about this; it is interesting for example to see a neuroscientist such as Edelman (1992) inveighing against the biologically unrealistic assumptions of AI. Interesting also to see Tipler (1994) using the assumptions of AI to promise us some kind of immortality through computer representations of our personalities. The fact that there are such divergent views in the scientific community perhaps gives theology more room for manoeuvre than is sometimes imagined.

There is often a tendency in many theological circles to side with social imperialism, and largely to discount the biological aspects of human nature. A good recent example of a theological view of human persons that emphasises the relational context of personhood is McFadyen's *The Call to Personhood* (1990). Though it is a valuable contribution to understanding the social aspects of personhood, it neglects the biological aspects of human nature, as does much theological anthropology in this tradition.

On the other hand, there is a separate tradition of theological thinking that emphasises the importance of physical embodiment to being human. In recent years, Nelson's *Embodiment* (1978) was an important contribution to this line of thinking, and it has also been important in feminist theology. However, in theology as in psychology, there is often not much contact between strands of theological thinking about personhood that emphasise the relational and the bodily aspects of being human.

The role of theologians in this warfare between biological and social imperialism is to oppose extremism. The natural world from which we have emerged is God's creation, and we belong to it. There is nothing in the Christian agenda that wishes to minimize that. On the other hand, the social world in which we live is also enormously important, especially the moral community within which we learn how to conduct ourselves, and the community of faith within which we learn salvation.

It seems to have been relatively rare for theologians to seek to integrate social and biological aspects of the human condition. One important recent exception is Farley's book *Good and Evil* (1990), which considers the social and interhuman as well as the personal and biological. I would suggest that breadth such as that is desirable in all theological reflection on being human. Perhaps those of us who are concerned with the scientific context in which theology must now operate, and who are aware of the importance of holding together the biological and social in the scientific study of human beings, can offer a corrective to the unbalanced view of human beings that often prevails within the theological community.

Evolution, Emergence and the Purposes of God

From a theological point of view, I would want to emphasise both the continuity of human beings with the natural world, and our transcendence from it. Often the tradition has not kept this balance well. There has been more emphasis on difference, on our unique *imago dei* status, than on continuity with the natural world. I would want to talk about how, in human beings, the natural and spiritual worlds meet; we are both natural and spiritual creatures, and in this sense stand at the hinge of creation.

One twentieth-century theologian who I think gets the balance right on this is Karl Rahner (1978). He sees the 'transcendent' or spiritual aspects of being human as arising from our natural creatureliness, and sees this as reflecting the purpose of God, including his incarnational purpose. If there is a problem in Rahner's account, it lies in an apparent slide from low to high notions of spiritual or transcendent. However, he does hold together the natural and spiritual aspects of being human in a coherent way. For theology to fail to give a proper account of either the natural or the spiritual aspects of being human obscures our pivotal place in God's creative purposes.

Note that neither Rahner nor I are talking about our being the pinnacle of creation, or of our being somehow perfect; neither am I necessarily talking of our uniqueness in this regard. We seem to be unique among earth creatures, but I make no assumptions about whether or not elsewhere in the universe there might be creatures like ourselves that are both natural and spiritual.

I am using 'spiritual' here as a shorthand for the ways in which human beings differ from other higher animals, but the term needs more explication. We need to be conscious of the trend in biological anthropology to emphasise the continuity of human beings with the rest of the animal kingdom. I am not trying to say that there is something so unique about human beings that it has no roots whatsoever in the other species from whom we have evolved; that would be biologically implausible. For example, our kind of consciousness, especially our distinctive kind of self-consciousness, has its roots in the kinds of consciousness also found in animals. However, it would be flying in the face of common sense to say that human beings do not manifest capacities which are developed to a new and distinctive degree.

Suggesting that the development of spiritual creatures like ourselves represents 'God's creative purposes' may be seen to be buying into a teleological view of evolution of a kind that would be disowned by most evolutionary biologists. I do not assume that evolution proceeded along a fixed track that would in principle have been predictable had there been anyone around to make the predictions. Neither do I even necessarily assume that it was God's purpose and intention that it should proceed in exactly the way it did. However, I do assume that there are such advantages in our kind of highly developed capacity for information processing that it was likely that creatures with such capacities would develop somehow or other in the end; though they need not have been exactly like ourselves, and they need not have evolved by exactly the route that we did. I also assume that it was God's intention and purpose that, in this way, creatures should emerge that were capable of conscious relationship to him.

Every evolutionary biologist knows that capacities may underpin a variety of different functions. Capacities that develop because of one particular advantage in the battle for survival may turn out fortuitously to underpin a much broader range of functions. Our special capacities were presumably selected initially because they helped our ancestors to survive, but having come into existence they also subserve our likeness to God and our capacity to form a relationship with him. However, we should perhaps be wary of assuming that evolutionary biology can provide us with an adequate account of how and why our spiritual capacities evolved.

There are interesting trends in evolutionary theory to note here. For example, Varela and his colleagues, in their excellent book *The Embodied Mind* (1992) seek to release us from the tyranny of the Darwinian determinism that is inclined to argue that the characteristics of species can be adequately explained in terms of their selection advantage in the battle for survival. Varela *et al.*, among other recent evolutionary thinkers, emphasise the role of the self-organising capacities of creatures. Also, what survives is not necessarily what is *best* for survival, rather that a wide range of characteristics may be selected provided they do not work *against* survival.

The insight here is rather like Karl Popper's insight that we don't prove good scientific theories, it is just that our best theories survive disproof. In a similar way the characteristics that are retained through evolution are not necessarily those that have been specifically selected, but the much more diverse range of characteristics that were not eliminated because they worked against survival. There is a powerful warning here against expecting too much from evolutionary psychology. Its initial enthusiasts seem to have failed to learn the lessons of scientific history, and to be claiming that they can deliver more than is credible. It is unlikely that it will be possible to produce a complete explanation of why humans have the characteristics they do in terms of the survival advantage of those characteristics.

I have said that I am using the concept of the 'spiritual' as a way of referring to the capacities that differentiate us from other animals, capacities that critically, from a Christian point of view, enable us to relate to God. Various lists have been produced of such characteristics (Anderson 1998). Calling them 'spiritual' may seem to imply that they are wholly good, that they put us on the side of the angels, but I do not assume that. Our higher capacities are in fact highly ambivalent in their moral and spiritual implications.

For example, the self-consciousness that enables us to meditate and pray also enables us to worry and give ourselves insomnia. (Other animals do not have insomnia; it is a unique human achievement.) Our greater moral awareness is also ambivalent. We have a unique capacity to do good to others. Though sociobiologists like to use the term 'altruism' for any piece of animal behaviour that happens to benefit others, this is an abuse of the term, as Midgley (1985) and others have pointed out. Only moral creatures can properly be said to be altruistic. But if altruism is a unique human achievement, so is sin. Animals may do harm to one another, but you need moral awareness to do it in the deliberate way that counts as sin.

The myth in Genesis 3 that we call 'the fall' is an early reflection on these matters. The heart of the fall is not sin, but knowledge of good and evil, as James Barr points out in his recent book on the Garden of Eden (1992). Because it is not credible to take the story of the Fall literally, most people now take it ontologically as referring to the inherent wickedness of human beings. However, it seems to me perfectly possible to take it in a roughly historical way, as referring in mythological form to the acquisition of the knowledge of good and evil that must have occurred as *Homo Sapiens* evolved. This development of moral awareness is ambivalent in its implications. The new consciousness of human beings can lead to the sin that features in the myth of the fall, but it also leads to the great achievements of human beings, and ultimately to the possibility of the incarnation. In the latter sense it is, as many have said, a 'fall upwards'.

In talking about the ambivalent moral impact of the capacities that differentiate us from other animals, I am also implicitly taking a similar view of the moral ambivalence of our animal inheritance and emphasising that it is not all bad. There has been a tendency in some circles to associate our animal inheritance with what is bad in us. Indeed, Campbell (1975) equates original sin with our animal inheritance and sees this as being set against the good qualities that come from our distinctively human capacities. This is also to fail to see the morally ambivalent nature of what is distinctly human (see also Hefner 1993, ch. 8).

Scientific thought comes in layers. There is a layer that is very close to empirical data, where ideology is least evident, but there are higher levels of scientific thought which deal with general world-views (i.e. with metaphysics) and which often float rather loosely over the empirical data. It is these higher levels of scientific thought that raise theological issues most clearly, and with which theologians most need to engage. One of the chief obstacles to such a dialogue is the reluctance of scientists to recognize that they are often dealing with age-old myths in slightly modified form; so a helpful first step is to recognize the religious myths that sometimes stand behind apparently scientific world-views. There is a danger of trying to put a theological gloss on modern scientific myths about the human person without first analysing how some of these scientific myths have been stolen from theology in the first place, albeit twisted a bit in the process.

The close relationship between the biblical myth of the fall and Dawkins' modern myth of the Selfish Gene illustrates very well the close but concealed relationship there can be between theological and scientific world-views. Goodwin, in his *How the Leopard Changed its Spots* (1994), makes some interesting remarks about how the sociobiological myth of the selfish gene is basically the Christian myth of original sin in naturalized form. The old idea that we are born sinful resurfaces as the claim that our hereditary material is basically selfish; then the idea that our sinful nature condemns us to a life of conflict and toil resurfaces as the idea that our selfish genes lead to competitive interaction and to the constant attempt to reach competitive advantage over rivals in the fitness stakes. Finally, as Dawkins says, because we are born selfish, we will have to learn to be altruistic, which corresponds to the religious idea that there can be salvation from our selfish nature. Looked at in this way, you can easily spot that though Dawkins tries to retain something corresponding to salvation in his Darwinian myth, he does not have the resources to do this convincingly; he has no good account of how altruism is to be learned, or why it should be.

The standard form of biological thinking about how our distinctive human capacities have emerged is that they result from the increasing complexity of the central nervous system, and the information-processing capacities that arise from it. It is worth pausing, however, to note the social constructivist critique that can be offered of that kind of story. We tend perhaps to make oversharp distinctions between genes and environment in the evolutionary process, and between the organism and the environment. Though these distinctions are helpful first approximations, they can be misleading if we hold to them too rigidly.

Oyama, in her *Ontogeny of Information* (1985), has criticized the distinction between genes and environment as an artificial and misleading one. Goodwin (1994) has made similar points. Everyone knows that human characteristics such as intelligence are part 'nature', part 'nurture'. The point that now needs to be made is that you can't separate genes from the environment sufficiently to really be able to speak of what genes do as opposed to what the environment does. It is only a slight exaggeration to say that neither genes nor environment, on their own, have any effect whatsoever. It is the interaction between genes and environment that determines almost everything about us. Moreover, these interactive effects can take many forms, and can operate along many different developmental pathways; there is no invariant form of interaction between them.

In a similar way, Varela *et al.* (1992) argue against an over-strong separation between organism and environment, just as we need to avoid an over-rigid separation of genes from environment. The environment that is important from most points of view is the *perceived* environment. Of course, there are constraints on this perceived environment; we cannot simply fantasise any environment we like. However, it is the environment as we perceive it that we adapt to; perceiving features of the environment opens up possibilities for adaptation that would not be present if we were oblivious of them.

This view of things underlines how radically different is the adaptation of human beings to their environment from that of any other species. We live in what Varela *et al.* call an 'enacted' environment to a greater degree than any other creatures. Many of the ways in which we enact our world are socially shared and culturally transmitted. There are individual elements of course, but the collective determination is very strong. These considerations should give pause to a biological imperialism that wishes to explain the social and psychological features of human beings in terms of evolution; against that has to be set the fact that for human beings, the environment within which evolution takes place is to a large degree socially constructed and enacted.

Natural and Social Science

These considerations bring us to the general issue of how to relate naturalistic and social approaches within the sciences. Psychology is particularly interesting here because of the diverse approaches to the human person that fall within it. At one end of the spectrum, psychology is a biological science, at the other it is a social science. There is always something of a tension between the two, and relatively few people conduct research on human functioning in a way that integrates both. Nevertheless, it seems to me enormously important that there should be a discipline that holds together these potentially disparate aspects of the study of human beings. If we did not have such a discipline, we would need to construct one; but we have it already, and it is called psychology (Watts 1992).

Sadly, in practice, psychology is often just an umbrella under which many strands of research, from the biological to the social, coexist under the same roof. But more than this is needed if we are to move towards a more adequate scientific understanding of what it is to be human. The first piece of ground-clearing for this is to reject the kind of imperialistic claims, by either the biological or the social end of psychology, that would make it impossible to have an integrated discipline that united both. Within psychology, there are strong forms of both biological determinism and social constructionism. It is the strong forms that are problematic; their weaker counterparts present no obstacle to a broad biological/social discipline. The phrase 'nothing but', or its equivalents, often gives the game away and indicates that strong forms are being espoused. In both the biological and the social case, I am happy to accept the non-exclusive claims of the weak reductionist positions, but firmly reject the more exclusive claims of the strong positions.

Take social contructionism (see Greenwood 1994). There is a weak form that points out that all the categories with which we understand human beings are social constructions, and in this sense are contingent. However, there is also a strong form of social constructionism that goes further and says that our personal life is 'nothing but' a social construction. That makes it irrelevant, misleading, illegitimate to study other aspects of emotions such as the biological ones. However, there is no basis whatsoever for asserting that our thoughts and feelings are 'nothing but' social constructions.

At the opposite end there is biological determinism, and one of the most influential forms of this at present is neurological determinism. Of course, the brain is involved in every aspect of human functioning. Except in the most basic reflex-like reactions, it is not bypassed. However, there is a strong form of neurological determinism that would go further and say that our emotions, thoughts and personalities are 'nothing but' what goes on in our brains, that we are 'just a bundle of neurones' as Francis Crick (1994) put it (see Watts 1994 for a critique of Crick).

There are a variety of interlinked claims that tend to go together here, though they can in principle be detached from one another:

(*a*) One is that higher-level phenomena such as mind can be explained 'completely' in terms of lower-level ones such as brain. It is worth emphasising how hypothetical this concept of complete explanation is. In the human sciences everything is so complex and interlinked that there are probably no examples of complete explanations of anything. In this situation, it is curious that so much debate is given to the implications of achieving a complete explanation if that were ever possible. It is a debate about an entirely hypothetical scenario, and one that is most unlikely to ever occur. Though it is complete biological explanations that are most often considered, very similar issues arise about the idea of complete social explanations.

(*b*) Another rather different kind of claim is that higher-level phenomena have no causal influence, that they are mere 'epiphenomena' that float on the surface and do no causal work. This is also a curious claim. Though it is very difficult to assess empirically, it seems unlikely to be correct. For example, it *does* seem as though it makes a difference whether or not people become consciously aware of something. Of course, that is not conclusive, because it is always possible to claim that consciousness of something has particular effects because of the distinct brain processes associated with it. This leads to the other oddity of the idea that causal work is done entirely at lower levels. This is the attempt to divorce high and low levels completely, prior to specifying at which level the causal work is being done. The problem here is that the concept of the person gets obliterated. As Midgley emphasises in her chapter, *we* do things, not our minds or brains; there is something odd about trying to suggest that our minds have no place in this causal work. Minds and brains are too intertwined for it to be reasonable to suggest that causal work is done entirely by brains, and not at all by minds.

(*c*) Third, there are suggestions that higher-level processes are in some sense not 'real'. It is never clear what is meant by this. 'Real' is a strange word, and what is meant by it in any context depends on what it is being contrasted with, and it is not clear what might possibly be meant by saying that high-level processes such as mind or personality are in some sense not 'real'. I suggest that if this claim were spelt out clearly, it would be evident that our minds and personalities are not 'unreal' in any convincing way. This is probably the aspect of reductionism that is most relevant to the theology of the person; a Christian view would certainly want to maintain the reality of the higher aspects of ourselves.

I would also reject any claims to 'primacy' by one particular aspect of human beings. Claims to primacy arise in relation to phenomena such as depression, which is an interesting example of a complex multifaceted human phenomenon. Some people think that the social circumstances within which depression arises are primary; other people think that the biological aspects are primary. To say that one aspect of depression is primary is to claim that it comes first and explains all the others. However, this is not how human beings work. Our social circumstances affect what goes on in our bodies; equally our physiological state and brain processes affect our social functioning. I believe that all claims to primacy are spurious, and that human beings are too systemic for such claims to be credible.

These are all controversial issues within the human sciences, and among philosophers, and I have taken a particular position about them which not everyone would accept. I have also deliberately raised the issues in as non-technical a way as possible, because I have come to feel that the way these matters are currently being debated among philosophers obscures what is at stake theologically rather than elucidating it.

Part of the difficulty in integrating the biological and social aspects of the study of human beings within psychology is the way in which psychology is both a natural science dealing with the biological aspects of human beings, and a social science dealing with the relational aspects of being human. In recent decades (stemming from Winch 1958), there has been a developing philosophy of social science that emphasises how it differs from the natural sciences, for example in being more concerned with reasons for actions than with causes. The distinction between natural and social science reflects the basic distinction between two different kinds of concepts, natural kinds and social constructs (e.g. cabbages *v*. cities).

One of the key divergences, apart from this, between biological and social psychology is the amoral world assumed by biological psychology. It contrasts with the moral order which social psychology is increasingly willing to assume in explaining, for example, human emotions. This is a point at which there is also a divergence between natural science and theology. The basic assumption of natural science is that the world does not reflect any underlying moral purpose, whereas it is central to theology that it does assume a moral purpose underlying all reality. If psychology could successfully span the divide between an assumed moral and amoral context in its study of persons, it would be an achievement that would indirectly be of considerable importance for the relationship between natural science and theology.

Psychology is situated on the fault line between the natural and the social sciences. No surprise then that the discipline tends to fall apart, and some might argue that it is fruitless to try to continue with a discipline that is an uncomfortable hybrid between natural and social science. My own view is that human beings can never be understood if their natural (biological) and social (relational) aspects are kept separate, and that it is extremely important for the enterprise of understanding human nature that ways are found of pursuing naturalistic and social approaches in harmony with one another. The challenge psychology faces in holding its disparate wings together are of great importance in the broad intellectual context of our times.

I have already said that on theological grounds I would want to take a broad view of the human person that held together the social and the biological. It would also be helpful for the relationship between natural science and theology if strong links were forged between the naturalistic approach to the person of biological psychology and the more hermeneutic approach of social psychology. That could set helpful precedents for the interlinking of the natural sciences and the hermeneutic discipline of theology.

References

ANDERSON, E. 1998. 'A Genetic view of Human Nature', in W. Brown *et al.* (eds), *Whatever Happened to the Soul?: Scientific and Theological Portraits of Human Nature*, Minneapolis: Fortress Press.

ANDERSON, R. S. 1982. *On Being Human: Essays in Theological Anthropology*, Grand Rapids: Eerdmans.

D'AQUILI, E. G. and NEWBERG, A. B. 1998. 'The neuropsychology of religion', in F. Watts (ed.), *Science Meets Faith*, London: SPCK.

BARR, J. S. 1992. *The Garden of Eden and the Hope of Immortality*, London: SCM Press.

BROWN, W. *et al.* (eds). 1998. *Whatever Happened to the Soul?: Scientific and Theological Portraits of Human Nature*, Minneapolis: Fortress Press.

CAMPBELL, D. T. 1975. 'The conflict between biological and social evolution and the concept of original sin', *Zygon* 10, 234–49.

CRICK, F. 1994. *The Astonishing Hypothesis: The Scientific Search for the Soul*, London: Simon & Schuster.

DE SOUSA, R. 1987. *The Rationality of Emotion*, Cambridge, Mass.: MIT Press.

DIXON, T. 1999. 'Theology, anti-theology and atheology: from theological passions to secular emotions', *Modern Theology* 15, 297–330.

EDELMAN, G. 1992. *Bright Air, Brilliant Fire*, London: Penguin Press.

FARLEY, E. 1990. *Good and Evil: Interpreting a Human Condition*, Minneapolis: Fortress Press.

GOODWIN, B. 1994. *How the Leopard Changed its Spots*, London: Weidenfeld & Nicolson.

GREENWOOD, J. D. 1994. *Realism, Identity and Emotion*, London: Sage.

HARRÉ, R. 1986. *The Social Construction of Emotions*, Oxford: Blackwell.

HEFNER, P. 1993. *The Human Factor: Evolution, Culture and Religion*, Minneapolis: Fortress Press.

VON HUGEL, F. 1923. *The Mystical Element of Religion as Studied in Saint Catherine of Genoa and her Friends*, 2nd edn, London: Dent.

JAMES, W. 1960. *The Varieties of Religious Experience*, London: Collins.

JEEVES, M. A. 1997. *Human Nature at the Millennium: Reflections on the Integration of Psychology and Christianity*.

KATZ, S. T. 1978. *Mysticism and Philosophical Analysis*, London: Sheldon Press.

LASH, N. 1988. *Easter in Ordinary*, London: SCM Press.

McFADYEN, P. 1990. *The Call to Personhood*, Cambridge: Cambridge University Press.

MIDGLEY, M. 1985. *Evolution as Religion*, London: Methuen.

MURPHY, N. 1998. 'Non-reductive physicalism', in W. Brown *et al.* (eds), *Whatever Happened to the Soul?: Scientific and Theological Portraits of Human Nature*, Minneapolis: Fortress Press.

NELSON, J. B. 1978. *Embodiment*. New York: Pilgrim Press.

OATLEY, K. 1992. *Best Laid Schemes: The Psychology of Emotion*, Cambridge: Cambridge University Press.

—— and JENKINS, J. M. 1996. *Understanding Emotions*, Oxford: Blackwell.

OYAMA, S. 1985. *The Ontogeny of Information*, Cambridge: Cambridge University Press.

PROUDFOOT, W. 1985. *Religious Experience*, Berkeley: University of California Press.

RAHNER, K. 1978. *Foundations of Christian Faith*, New York: Crossroad Press.

REED, E. 1997. *From Soul to Mind: The Emergence of Psychology from Erasmus Darwin to William James*, New Haven: Yale University Press.

SOLOMON, R. C. 1993. *The Passions: Emotions and the Meaning of Life*, 2nd edn, Indianapolis: Hackett.

TIPLER, F. 1994. *The Physics of Immortality*, Basingstoke: Macmillan.

VARELA, F. J., THOMPSON, E. and ROSCH, E. 1992. *The Embodied Mind: Cognitive Science and Human Experience*, Cambridge, Mass.: MIT Press.

WATTS, F. 1992. 'Is psychology falling apart?', *The Psychologist* 5, 489–94.

—— 1994. 'You're nothing but a pack of neurones', *Journal of Consciousness Studies* 1, 275–9.

—— 1997. 'Psychological and religious perspectives on emotion', *Zygon* 32, 243–60.

WATTS, F. 1998. 'Brain, mind and soul', in F. Watts (ed.), *Science Meets Faith*, London: SPCK.

WILLIAMS, J. M. G., WATTS, F. N., MACLEOD, C. and MATHEWS, M. 1997. *Cognitive Psychology and Emotional Disorders*, 2nd edn, Chichester: John Wiley.

WINCH, P. 1958. *The Idea of a Social Science*, London: Kegan Paul.

4

The Child's Brain – On Neurogenetic Determinism and Free Will

HUGO LAGERCRANTZ

In the present essay I shall argue that neurogenetic determinism is a modern version of the old preformation idea, which believed that there is a fully developed individual from the very beginning. The preformation idea assumes that development is merely a matter of scaling up. However, it is difficult to understand how about 40,000 genes can code for the wiring of 100 billions of neurons, each one with at least about a thousand dendrites and synapses. The brain of the newborn infant looks in fact more like a jungle than a computer. According to one theory the organization of the brain occurs by group selection or neuronal Darwinism, i.e. the most useful or strongest neurons survive while the others disappear. 'Neurons which fire wire, while neurons which do not fire go to the sink.' In this way sensory input can form or at least influence the development of the brain. Thus development is epigenetic; many different components have to come together at the right place and time.

Neurogenetic Determinism?

Genes encoding for depression, novelty-seeking, absolute pitch and homosexuality have been discovered during the last decade.

Recently a gene encoding for alcoholism was transferred to the fruit fly, which got addicted to this very human fluid. The drunken fly was created by human beings. The question is now whether we can predict not only future diseases, but also the behaviour or personality of the newborn infant on a genetic basis. Is it like in the old tales, when the fairy present at the birth predicted the fate of the newborn prince or princess?

Thus we are asking the eternal question about the free will, but in a modern molecular biological context. 'We are just survival machines – robot vehicles blindly programmed to preserve the selfish molecules known as genes', according to Richard Dawkins (1976), a famous author of popular science. Neurogenetic determinism is the modern version of the preformation idea, i.e. the *homunculus* in the head of the sperm just expands to become a human being. The hardline molecular geneticists seem to be the preformation believers of our time.

One main argument raised by (for example) the French neurobiologist Jean-Pierre Changeux (1997) against the neurogenetic determinism is that the human genome contains 'only' about 40,000 genes which are involved in the formation of the brain, but the brain contains about 100 billions of neurons. Each neuron may have 1000 to 10,000 synapses connecting with other neurons. Thus there is not sufficient information in the human genome for the wiring of these complex networks. If there is not a sufficient number of genes to govern the hardware, it is difficult to understand how there could be enough information to encode for the software, i.e. the behaviour. To understand this complexity we need a further look at how the human brain is developed.

Formation of the Neural Tube

According to the British embryologist Lewis Wolpert (1997) the most important event during life is not birth or marriage but gastrulation. This is the event when the three-dimensional individual is formed from the amorphous mass of cells. If there is no gastrulation we would remain flatworms. During this phase the cranial–caudal axis is formed by induction mediated by a rod-like structure, the notochord. This was discovered in the 1920s when the German professor Hans Spemann together with his graduate student Hilde Mangold transplanted a little piece of a salamander embryo containing the notochord. In this way they were able to create a two-headed embryo. This was a remarkable discovery, for which Spemann received the Nobel Prize in medicine or physiology for 1935.

Spemann's factor is still frequently discussed in journals like *Nature, Science* and *The Cell*. Spemann's contribution to our understanding of human thinking today is probably more important than that of his more famous colleague in Freiburg, Martin Heidegger. Some of the genes involved in this early formation of the brain have been retained during evolution since 600 million years ago, when the insects and the vertebrates started to develop along separate branches. These genes are called homeotic genes, for example the hog genes. These genes determine what should be the front or the end of the nervous system. If these genes are transplanted to the rear part of the fruit fly, antennae will grow out besides the back legs.

One of the most important genes in this early formation of the brain are the so-called hedgehog genes, named after a popular video play. The hedgehog gene determines for example which neurons should develop to motor neurons in the spinal cord controlling muscle movements. If this gene is knocked out, all neurons will become sensory neurons by default pathway. The hedgehog gene has a number of functions during early brain development. How do these early immature nerve cells know how to differentiate? The concentration of the inducing substance seems to be important. If the cells are exposed to a high concentration of the substance they will become other cells than they would if they were exposed to low levels. An analogy proposed by Lewis Wolpert (1997) is that the cells constitute bits of a French flag. Each cell has the potential to turn blue, white, or red. Whether these bits should become blue, white or red is determined by the distance from the flag pole, i.e. the concentration gradient.

Proliferation of Neurons

The next step in brain development is the proliferation of new neurons. About 200,000 new neurons are formed every minute between the eighth and eighteenth gestational weeks. This enormous cell multiplication occurs in the ventricles. The neurons migrate and form six layers. The newest nerve cells migrate to the outer layer. When a nerve cell has found its final position it does not divide more. After five months of pregnancy very few new nerve cells are formed, except possibly in the olfaction center and the cerebellum. Thus when we are born we have essentially all the nerve cells we are going to live with for the rest of our lives. The fact that most nerve cells are formed after the eighth and before the eighteenth gestational week we learned in a tragic way; fetuses which were exposed to the first atom bombs in Hiroshima and Nagasaki during this period of pregnancy became microcephalic, a condition which did not affect fetuses who were younger or older during these events.

Other animals like the canarian male birds seem to generate new nerve cells in the singing center during the mating spring season. The number of syllables they perform seems to be directly related to the number of neurons. However, humans do not seem to have this wonderful capacity. As Pasco Rakic (who discovered the migration of neurons) stated at a meeting: 'If I would be able to replace my neurons in my brain's speech center for talking I would be able to get rid of my Croatian accent when I speak English.'

The newly formed neurons migrate along a fan-like scaffold of glial threads. From each neuron an axon and a number of dendrites are formed. The nerves start to connect with each other. The wiring of the nervous system begins in the third fetal month and continues the rest of the life. According to Gerald Edelman (1992), the brain resembles more a jungle than a computer, particularly at this stage. The crucial question is now how the brain is organized and how the neurons find their way to their targets. As stated in an editorial in *Nature,* finding the interstate ways between New York and San Francisco is relatively easy compared to finding the way from the motor cortex to the end of the toes.

Organization of the Brain

If you look at the brain of a newborn baby in a microscope it does not look more primitive than the adult brain. Indeed it looks much more complicated, with billions of neurons, each one with thousands of arborizations and synapses. To organize the brain a number of neurons, dendrites and synapses must be eliminated. Actually nearly half of all the neurons which are formed in the fetus disappear in early infancy. This process is called apoptosis and is a general biological phenomena. For example, from the beginning we have paws with swimming skin between the digits. To form fingers and toes, the tissue between the digits disappears by apoptosis.

How this organization of the brain occurs is controversial. Gerald Edelman (1992) claims that the organization of the brain occurs by a so-called group selection according to a so-called neuronal Darwinism, i.e. the most useful or strongest neurons survive and develop while the others disappear. Neurons which fire wire while neurons which do not fire go to the sink, i.e. neurons which seem to make useful connections and are active form more dendrites and synapses, while others disappear. This explains in a nice way how the neuronal pathways between for example the eyes and the visual cortex develop, while pathways between for example the olfaction center and visual cortex disappear.

Some criticism of this theory has been raised. As stated by Changeux (1997), it is also possible that 'activity does not create novel connections, but rather, contributes to the elimination of preexisting ones'. For him, 'to learn is to eliminate'. The importance of stimulating the brain at an early age was discovered by David Hubel and Torsten Wiesel, who won the Nobel Prize in 1981 for this discovery. They found that when the eyes of a kitten were covered during a critical period in early life, the animals became blind. If the eyes are covered in an adult cat even for a very long time, the cat immediately sees, when the cover is removed. These findings showed that it is crucial to stimulate the infant brain during certain time periods – windows of opportunity. This finding has also had some important clinical implications. Infants who are born with cataract or certain types of squint must be operated on early, otherwise they can become blind.

The question is whether there is any stimulation of the fetal brain in the womb. The fetus can certainly feel the touch when it is kicking against the uterine wall. This feeling has been assumed to play some role for the formation of the sensory–motor arcs. It can also hear, smell and taste and feel pain. But what about the vision? There is not much to see. However, Carla Shatz at the University of Berkeley discovered that there is a high spontaneous activity in the retina of the ferret fetus. These waves of activity might simulate visual impressions – it is like running video films to teach the fetus to see. This activity is also recorded in the visual cortex. If this activity is blocked by a special drug (tetrodotoxin), the ferrets will become unable to see. Thus the function of the organ creates the organ as proposed by Lamarck. This Lamarckian constructivism has been presented as an alternative to Darwinian selectionism (Purves *et al.* 1996).

Plasticity of the Fetal and Infant Brain

About one of four very-low-birthweight infants (below 1000 grams) suffers from some sort of cerebral stroke, sometimes very severe. If the brains are studied by a magnetic resonance camera later in life, big cavities in the brain can be found. In spite of that the child may have developed normally, or nearly normally. This finding illustrates that there is great plasticity in the developing brain. Even if a great number of nerve cells are destroyed, others can take over and compensate for the deficits. However, it is important to stimulate these brain-damaged pre-term infants. A number of studies have shown that if these children are well-supported by their parents or other care-givers, they can often develop normally, while a combination of very pre-term birth and a psychologically and socially deprived environment results in a worse outcome for these children.

Neurogenetic Determinism Revisited

As stated by Changeux in *Neuronal Man* (1997), 'Recognizing the power of the genes in no way forces us to submit to their supreme authority'. The genome is relatively simple while the brain, particularly the human brain, is very complex. The discovery of a number of genes determining diseases and human behavior may result in some form of social defeatism. Books like Richard F. Herrnstein's *The Bell Curve* claiming that blacks and poor people are born with lower intelligence might even lead to racism and fascism. Our efforts to detect a special violence gene should not, for example, inhibit the forces to prohibit weapons in the United States. It is still probably much easier to decrease the availability of vodka than to knock out the alcoholic gene among Russians (if there is an alcoholic gene at all) (see Rose 1995). The typical example how we can overcome the power of the genes is the classical pediatric disease: phenyl-ketonuria. Infants suffering this lack a special gene which results in severe mental retardation. If this disease is detected by a general test performed in most countries, these children can eat a special diet lacking the dangerous amino acid and develop normally. If we can overcome the power of this very strong genetic trait, we should be able to overcome the influence of a number of genes determining various types of non-desirable hereditary properties (Lagercrantz *et al.* 1997). The brain has a strong plasticity, and it is important to utilize the critical windows to teach genetically impaired children languages, mathematics, music, reading and other good sides of life. I believe we have the free will to do this and can overcome the power of neurogenetic determinism.

References

CHANGEUX, J.-P. [1985] 1997. *Neuronal Man*, Princeton: Princeton University Press.

DAWKINS, R. 1976. *The Selfish Gene*, Oxford: Oxford University Press.

EDELMAN, G. 1992. *Bright Air and Brilliant Fire*, New York: BasicBooks.

LAGERCRANTZ H., APERIA, A., RITZEN M. and RYDELIUS P. A. 1997. 'Genetic versus Environmental Determinism of Human Behaviour and Health', *Acta Paediatrica* 86, suppl. 422.

Purves D., White, L. E. and Riddle D. R. 1996. 'Is Neuronal Development Darwinian?', *TINS* 19, 460–4.

Rose, S. 1995. 'The Rise of Neurogenetic Determinism', *Nature* 373, 380–2.

Wolpert, L. 1997. *Principles of Development*, Oxford: Oxford University Press.

5

Imago Dei:
The Possibility and Necessity
of the Human Person

PHILIP HEFNER

Introduction

Thesis, in preliminary form: The human person has emerged within the process of physical and biological evolution as a set of dynamics, enabled finally by the emergence of the human brain, in interaction with its world, including the culture of that world. To be a person involves organizing motivational urges (Sharif 1968) and integrating a wide range of feelings, ideas, intuitions, and evaluations (Sanford 1968). In other words, personhood is achieved through our acting upon the physical, biological and cultural materials that we have inherited, so as to establish a center of identity that shapes those materials into an understanding of the self, an understanding of the self's relation to the world in which it lives and to the people in that world, and into a life that holds itself accountable to those understandings of self, other people, and world. The person consequently emerges as both bio-logical and cultural. The Christian faith provides information for the guidance of the cultural dimension of person-formation. The Christian concept of humans created in the image of God is a way of grounding both the possibility of the person and also the necessity to which the person is accountable. The content of the image of God meme is that we become persons in our relationship to the whole of the world, through openness and accountability to the world, to its end, and to the Thou in community. This is in fact a relationship with God, and this proposal stands in contrast to definitions of person that focus primarily on conscious spiritual individuality.

I will elaborate this thesis in two parts, one of which focuses on certain elements of scientific thought, and the other on theological considerations.

Scientific Assumptions

My proposals concerning the concept of person rest on three assumptions drawn from scientific considerations: a physicalist assumption, an evolutionary assumption, and a cultural assumption (or rather, an assumption about culture).

The Physicalist Assumption

Whatever it means to be a person is rooted in the brain and its body. There can be little doubt about this. Person is what the human body/brain can become. Being a person involves the basic equipment of brain and body, and that equipment supports being person, it is not alien from or contrary to being a person. At the same time, our personhood is constrained by our body and its brain. This means that the physics of body and brain, as well as the genetics and the neurobiology of brain and body shape our personness in critical ways. Furthermore, there seems to be considerable correlation between the activities and states of the person and observable processes in the brain and body.

In this physicalist assumption, I can accept the work of neuroscientists and geneticists. These include Francis Crick's insistence that consciousness involves the neurons (1994); Gerald Edelman's argument that the mind cannot be understood in the absence of biology (1992); Michael Gazzaniga's description of the mind emerging through selection processes (1992); Eugene d'Aquili's and Andrew Newberg's reports of how meditation and mystical experience appear on a brain scan (1993) – if such hypotheses are confirmed by a consensus among researchers in the field, I see no reason to question them or to fear them.

I will argue, however, that if it is true to say that understanding what it means to be person is dependent on physicalist assumptions, it is equally true to say that other kinds of assumptions, some of them scientific in character, are also called for.

The Evolutionary-Emergent Assumption

The person has emerged within a set of evolutionary processes and is itself a process of emergence. On the one hand, the physical equipment that makes personhood possible is the fruit of millions of years of evolution. These processes have followed the dynamics that are generally associated with evolution, including the processes of adaptation to the environment and selection. Our genetic and neurobiological nature proceeds within us along Darwinian lines.

We may call these processes Darwinian, if that term is allowed to be a dynamic one. Some recent work has indicated that the processes described by the so-called complexity sciences are particularly relevant to the emergence of the human brain (Waldrop 1992; Deacon 1997). Complexity is described as processes in which a 'great many independent agents are interacting with each other in a great many ways,' so as to 'allow the system as a whole to undergo spontaneous self-organization,' perhaps even autopoeisis; furthermore, these processes of complexity are adaptive (Waldrop 1992, 11–12). Complex systems have been characterized as 'edge of chaos' phenomena, described as occurring in an abstract phase transition, a region of physical reality between the two extremes of order and chaos, where there is a 'certain kind of balance between the forces of order and the forces of disorder' (Waldrop 1992, 293; see also Kauffman 1995; Ashbrook and Albright 1997; Brun 1994, 1999; Gregersen 1998).

At the same time, we say that the person is an emergent within these evolutionary processes. Emergence has been defined in this way: 'When two entities are combined at a higher level of integration, not all the properties of the new entity are necessarily a logical or predictable consequence of the properties of the components' (Mayr 1988, 34–5). Emergence allows us to understand how something new can emerge within physical-biological processes while still not contravening natural processes. Complexity theory, as I have described it above, is an intensification of the theory of emergence.

Personhood not only is an emergent in the sense I have just described, but it is itself a process of emergence. A person is not a substance or an entity that we perceive as a thing. A person is like an eddy in a stream, a vital locus of centering in the flow of all that enters a human's system: the physics and chemistry, the biology, the psychology, the culture that enter into each of us, and their relevant history as well. Without necessarily accepting his detailed analysis or his specific terms, I am taking over a basic conceptuality from theologian Paul Tillich. He speaks of the multidimensional unity of life, incorporating in humans the evolved constellation of a number of dimensions, which he names as the inorganic, the organic, the animal, the self-aware, the psychological and the spiritual. The person is the creation of the spirit, as it works at centering the conditioning materials that emanate from this multidimensional unity. This conditioning material includes, for example, our specific body chemistry – genome, hormones, enzymes, and the like – as well as our psychology – drives, inclinations, emotions, desires – and our culture – childhood upbringing, ethnicity, social class placement, education, historical epoch, etc. To be a person is to engage in the struggle to center this vast array of conditioning material, so as to form a coherent self. As Tillich reminds us, the personal center is not identical with the conditioning material or any part of it, nor is it another element added to them. The personal center is furthermore not alien to the conditioning material, since it is in fact their center; the person is the conditioning material that constitutes it, under the conditions of centeredness (Tillich 1963, 17–30).

It may seem unusual to cite a theologian to express the scientific concept of evolutionary emergence, but I think that Tillich has stated this concept in a way that is particularly forceful and useful for us. The centering effort that he speaks of could be stated more antiseptically as psychologist Sharif does, when he says that the self is involved in the 'operation of motivational urges,' integrating processes of 'regulating, judging, perceiving, learning, remembering, thinking, planning, and decision making' (Sharif 1968, 151–9).

Assumptions Concerning Culture

Since person emerges in the context of the brain, it is not only a physical and biological phenomenon, but also cultural. By this I mean that the information inputs that are significant for the formation of personhood are not only physical and biological, but cultural. That is, they are inputs that derive from learning and teaching, within symbol systems that have been created to interpret and justify the inputs. The person, as Tillich describes it, is a construction, a construction at the physical and biological level, but also at the cultural level.

There is widespread agreement among neuroscientists that culture is a basic element in the formation of the person, along with the neurobiological factors. This recognition of culture as a component in the process of person-formation is a critical point for my discussion. Culture as I have defined it, although it emerges within a fully evolutionary biological context, introduces important new factors in the consideration of the concepts of person and of self, and thereby carries the evolutionary biological in new directions that require different kinds of maps for our understanding.

The Pivot of Culture: Memes, Spirit, and Theology

Culture accentuates the nature of the person as a phenomenon of organization and construction. I introduce this pivotal move in the discussion with a long quotation from Daniel Dennett. He writes:

> *What we are* is very much a matter of what culture has made us. Now we must ask how this all got started. What sort of evolutionary revolution happened that set us apart so decisively from all the other products of genetic revolution? (1995, 340)

Dennett begins with the story of how eukaryotic cells derived from procaryotes. He then continues: eukaryotic cells opened up the Vast space of possibilities we know as multicellular life, a space previously unimaginable. . . . Then a few billion years passed, while multicellular life forms explored various nooks and crannies of Design Space until, one fine day, another invasion began, in a single species of multicellular organism, a sort of primate, which had developed a variety of structures and capacities that just happened to be particularly well suited for these invaders. It is not surprising that the invaders were well adapted for finding homes in their hosts, since they were themselves created by their hosts, in much the way spiders create webs and birds create nests. In a twinkling – less than a hundred thousand years – these new invaders transformed the apes who were their unwitting hosts into something altogether new: *hosts*, who, thanks to their huge stock of newfangled invaders, could imagine the here-tofore unimaginable; leaping through Design Space as nothing had ever done before. Following Dawkins, I call the invaders *memes*, and the radically new kind of entity created when a particular sort of animal is properly furnished by – or infested with – memes is what is commonly called a person. (1995, 341)

I interject here the ironic observation that although Dennett and Dawkins are, by their own admission, hard reductionist thinkers, neither one friendly to religion, by introducing culture and memes as essential for human evolution and personhood, they admit an element into their thinking that renders their own reductionism wholly contradictory. I hope that my comments here will make that clear. A great deal of the scientific literature leapfrogs directly from physics, biology, genetics, and neurobiology, right over culture, to make judgements about the human mind and the behavior that it organizes and directs (see Atkins 1987; Edelman 1992; Gazzaniga 1992). Even Dennett (1995), who speaks so vividly of memes, presents a thesis that in its constructive reach is essentially dismissive of culture. The consequence for these thinkers is that they fall into near-absurdity in describing human personhood.

With the emergence of culture and memes, which I define as a packet of cultural information, a number of other critical elements are introduced into our concept of person. This is an important element of the heuristic I am introducing for our consideration. I do this in order to call attention: (1) to the importance of culture and (2) to the fact that introducing culture into my argument is a scientific move. Cultural information, memes, must be subjected to the activities that Sharif enumerated: regulating, judging, perceiving, learning, remembering, thinking, planning and decision making. These activities underscore the presence within the human person of self-awareness, freedom, critical thinking, envisioning the future, recognizing feedback, and the ability to correct oneself.

It is not often enough noted that elements of determinism originating at the biochemical, genetic, and neurobiological levels are significantly modulated at the cultural level. After I have heard the presentation on genetic determinism and biochemical reductionism, I leave the lecture hall, and face a whole range of decisions as to how I shall spend my evening, spend my money, and fill out my schedule book. Even if I am as much a creature of determinism as the lecturers say, I must endure the struggle and discomfort of wrestling with any number of decisions for my life, just as if I possessed a modicum of freedom. This is because I am a creature of culture as much as a creature of biochemistry, and it is this that so much of the literature ignores. If genetics and the neurosciences are to realize their constructive significance for understanding what person means, they must give serious attention to their interface with the brain's capacity in which it receives culture, organizes its information into systems and behaves in response to that information.

Even if culture is on a so-called genetic leash, life on that leash entails judgements, choices, and response to feedbacks. Culture is not possible without the kind of freedom that culture necessitates. Of course, this freedom is identical neither to the classical liberal ideal of liberty nor to the classical Marxist ideal of the complete malleability of the world to human shaping. Elsewhere I have spoken of this freedom as the condition and ambiance for human existence (see Hefner 1993, 97–122). This insight is critical to our consideration of what it means to be person.

These activities are all undertaken with the view in mind of organizing the information received into a centeredness that can be acted upon and carried forward. Culture and centeredness thus introduce values, both moral and non-moral. These translate into behavior, which determines, among non-moral values, what is more useful, preferable, and likely to accomplish what we intend.

With respect to moral values, the issues of good and bad, 'ought' and 'ought not' come to the fore.

None of this language – judging, learning, thinking, planning, values, moral behavior – makes sense if culture is not a central reality for the person. Tillich considers the formation of the centered self to be the distinctive accomplishment for human beings. He calls it an achievement brought about by spirit – not necessarily God's Holy Spirit, the third person of the Trinity, but by the human spirit, which in turn is the point where we do relate to God's Spirit.

What I am concerned to say with special force at this point is that religion generally, and Christian faith and theology, specifically, are systems of memes, cultural information, that have played a fundamental role in the emergence of persons, and continue to make significant proposals for understanding today what it means to be person. The remaining portion of my presentation will focus on this point. This designation of religion, faith, and theology as systems of memes is a scientific judgement, and it is one that is quite conventional. From within the religious community itself, however, we speak in theological terms. These memes have to do with our basic myth and ritual, to use terms more congenial to anthropologists. Although these memes have emerged within the processes of cultural evolution, they cannot be accounted for. There is no research that I know of that has accounted empirically or historically for the emergence of myth and ritual. They have simply appeared, so far as we know, veiled in the mist of archaic history. In the Christian framework, we speak of these primal memes as revelation. The philosopher Arthur Danto is perhaps acknowledging this when he writes, echoing Strawson (1959), that the elusive origins of personhood compel us to speak of it as an 'ontologically primitive' idea that cannot be fully accounted for by rational analysis (Danto 1967, 110).

Faith and theology face the challenge to clarify the deepest meanings of their memes with respect to the concept of person and to recognize how these memes relate to the scientific knowledge that I have referred to. When they meet this challenge, faith and theology will be in a position to present their memes as a challenge to the scientific and secular perspectives on personhood and press for a deeper consideration of what it means to be person.

Person as Spiritual Individuality

In his reflections on science and technology, Paul Tillich pointed out many years ago that we are in great danger of phrasing the discussion in such a way that the deepest and most significant issues of human existence simply never appear on the screen (Tillich 1988). I believe that this is happening today with respect to discussions of brain, mind, and person. If mind is equated with brain, for example, and brain is exhaustively discussed in terms of neurochemical and evolutionary processes, the most basic issues that the human tradition has associated with mind are not so much disproven or rejected, they are simply denied a place in the discussion. Of course, the tradition of humanistic reflection often conspires in its own dismissal when it fails to discern the genuine depth of basic human concerns and issues.

A case in point is the widespread understanding that person is identical to spiritual individuality and its dynamics (see Pannenberg 1961, 230–2). I use the term 'spiritual' here in the sense of the German *geistig*. The closest we can get to this in English is either to use the term '*psychic*,' which says too little, or '*spiritual*,' which says perhaps too much. Although I disagree with his assumptions in this regard, I do find useful Tillich's own practice of referring to Spirit with an upper-case *S* in the case of God, and with a lower-case *s* to refer to the human spirit. In both cases, divine and human, spirit refers to *the power that renders meaning actual* (Tillich 1963, 22, 30–110).

Both Tillich and Wolfhart Pannenberg trace this concept of person as equivalent to spiritual individuality from ancient Western philosophy through the nineteenth century to the present (Tillich 1948, 121; Pannenberg 1961, 230–2; 1977, 16). At times, the processes of spiritual individuality were described as more rational, at other times as more emotional, and in times influenced by science, more psychological. Although it was often recognized, as modern psychology has, that the self is socially bestowed, as well as internally driven, the concepts of self and person derive from what goes on in the human spirit or psyche.

It is precisely these internal dynamics of the spiritual individuality that are on their way to being described in terms of scientific causal explanations. Consequently, as the thesis of Francis Crick's recent book (1994) illustrates (namely, that all our interior states are properties of our neurons), the situation Tillich feared has come to pass. The deepest human questions concerning the point of being a person, as well as questions of the self's purpose, are simply no longer in the lexicon that governs the discussion.

Michael Gazzaniga articulates this view in the context of contemporary neuroscience when he writes:

> an organism comes delivered to this world with all the complexity it will ever have already built into it. In the case of the modern brain, a range of circuits that enable a variety of behavioral and cognitive strategies become matched with an environmnental challenge and the selection process starts. What looks to be learning is in fact the organism searching through its library of circuits and accompanying strategies that will best allow it to respond to the challenge. When the concept, which is well established in basic biology, is applied to more integrative mechanisms of mind, it goes a long way in explaining not only complex phenomena such as learning, language acquisition, mental disease, and variations in intelligence, but also everyday patterns. (1992, 199–200)

James Watson, who received a Nobel Prize in 1962, along with Francis Crick, for discovering the structure of the DNA molecule, put it much more crudely than either Crick or Gazzaniga, when he suggested at a consultation on germline genetic engineering last month in California, that 'a very serious disease,' which he identified as 'stupidity,' could be cured by germline interventions (Kolata 1998, A12).

What Crick and Gazzaniga fail to take into account is that under the conditions of culture, on the one hand, the neurons of the *Homo sapiens* brain must be marshalled on behalf of unique judgements and decisions, and, on the other, that same *Homo sapiens* does not simply search through its library of circuits and strategies, but rather also faces the challenge first of all, of defining the challenge, and then of deciding whether and how circuits and strategies can meet it.

The issue at stake here is not whether the scientific causal explanations are necessarily wrong or to be disputed, nor whether they must be taken seriously into account for our reflections. Rather, the issue is whether we have made a mistake when we have defined person and self so as to be coterminous with the interior psychic processes that these scientific explanations cover. What we mean by person and self, by the organizing center of personhood, is not adequately described by the functioning of my cerebral equipment. Rather, *it is defined in its intercourse with the challenges it must face.* It is to this process of the person's definition that our scientific study ought also to be turned, and to which I now turn in this discussion.

In another context, we might conclude that even though sour cream is a fundamental ingredient for beef stroganoff, reflection on the latter is not exhausted by a complete understanding of sour cream. So, too, the genetics, neurobiology and psychology of the internal psychic process of my individuality are fundamental to my being a person, but there are other considerations to be taken into account as well. Although these considerations are no more essential to the person than the workings of spiritual individuality, they are just as integral to being a person.

The Grounding of Person in a Network of Relationships: God, World, the Thou

I begin with the reflections that I offered above when I noted the pivotal significance of the emergence of the human being as a biocultural creature, a creature of culture as well as of biology. My argument is that the very nature of our cultural existence brings us to the point where we meet what Tillich calls the 'unconditional demand' that addresses every person to actualize itself concretely in its world (1948, 118 ff.). Person-formation is not only constituted by physico-biological behavior, it is also at its very core an accomplishment of the self within its world. The accomplishment is also the actualization of what one's pre-personal vitality can become. It is not in fundamental opposition to the physico-biological antecedents of personhood, but rather a statement of

what they can become. This means that being a person is constituted both by a *cognitive process* of perceiving and understanding
oneself in one's world, and also by a *moral process* of responding in
relationship to that world. Formally, then, the person is defined in
relationships (Tillich 1963, 32–50). These relationships also possess
a material content, and they constitute a rich relational network.

Within these relationships that are marked by demand and
response, person is *a moral concept*. That is what the scientific causal
explanations leave out of consideration, and that is why they must
be taken up into a more adequate elaboration. I do not propose to
follow here a method of opposing the science nor to point to any of
its flaws – that is for scientists to do. Rather, I follow here the lead
of physicist Niels Bohr, when he said that 'the opposite of a correct
statement is a false statement. But the opposite of a profound truth
may well be another profound truth' (quoted by Wilson 1990, 245).
Pannenberg says something similar when he says that scientific
explanation is to be augmented and deepened, as theology takes
the measure of scientific explanations. My aim here is to point in
the direction of a profound truth that can take the measure of the
sciences that study the person.

What is the substance of the moral demand, in response to which
the person is defined? The substance is shaped by the sense of
having to establish or actualize one's personhood in the world in
which one exists. Thus a relationship to one's world is integral to
the formation of the person. But this actualization is also marked
by an over-againstness in relationship to the world. It is true on the
one hand that we belong to our world and it to us, but it is also true
that in making a demand upon us, the world is *other* to us. We are
shaped in our evolution by involvement in and with this world.
Within this involvement, our world is both nurturer and other.
Using the German concepts, we can say that the world is both *Gabe*
and *Aufgabe* for us.

What is the character of this other that we face in our world? It is
the world in its totality, in terms of both space and time. Of course,
we cannot comprehend the world in its empirical totality, but we
act on the assumption that we are in touch with the essential nature
of that totality. Our existence occurs in concrete places and events,

to be sure, but we instinctively try to relate the idiosyncrasies of our situations to the larger world. We make decisions, for example, to receive an education for ourselves or our children in specific schools located in specific places, but we pursue the education with an eye to its adequacy for life wherever we or our children may live. Similarly with temporal totality, we act in the present, but on behalf of the future, on behalf of what we can become in the totality of our lives. So with our example of education – whether for ourselves or for our children, we pursue the education with an eye on the future of what we shall and can become.

This situation in which we meet the demand of our world as other and define our personhood in response to that demand possesses ontological depth, at least in an operationally effective way in our actual living, if not in an explicit metaphysical system. Although we may be consciously aware of a provisionality in our understanding of our world and in our response to it, we cannot respond with a lack of seriousness. Even our sense of provisionality has a de facto ontological reality. Furthermore, we do not respond to this world only as if its demand were outside our selves, as if it were simply a tyrannical heteronomous agency that we must obey. We respond because we want to, because we know that our self-hood requires this venture in actualization. It is the call of our own personhood that we are heeding when we respond to the demand of our world. Some neuropsychologists have drawn attention to the fact that the human mind seems to work with a sense that it is part of something larger (Glassman 1996; Teske 1996). The theological framework I am proposing here is one way of conceptualizing this 'something larger.'

In other words, as Tillich would say, our response to our world, through which we are defined, has to do with our being or non-being, with ultimacy, and therefore it is a religious transaction, and our reflection upon it is theological.

Let us be clear about the nub of what I am arguing. To be a person is not fully contained in our physico-biological behavior, but rather also requires the marshalling of that behavior in response to the demand from our world to actualize our authentic possibilities within it. Our person is shaped, therefore, in the awareness of an other and the challenge which that other poses as the defining ambiance for actualizing our selfhood. Since this other turns out, in practice, to be grounded in ultimacy, the formation of our personhood is both a moral and a theological transaction.

I have just stated the process of person-formation in phenomenological terms, accessible to secular rationality. However, as a Christian theologian, I believe that the articulation is incomplete until it is given a theological rendition. Wolfhart Pannenberg has advanced the thesis that it is the Hebrew and Christian traditions that have contributed the fullest understanding of the concept of person (1961, 1977). He bases his thesis on the Hebrew and Christian descriptions of human life in relationship to the God who is over against us. A number of his specific insights are worth rehearsing here.

(1) We become persons, first of all, when we understand ourselves to be in the presence of a God who is personal agent. Pannenberg explicitly rejects the idea that human beings first conceived of themselves as persons and then projected that person-concept upon God. He invokes the religious experience of archaic peoples, in which the divine reality was conceived in terms of persons, and humans received their personhood because of their relation to the gods. This is distinct from the question whether human attributes were projected onto the gods. It was in the experience of contingent events, and in the belief that there was some unity in those events, that humans came to the notion that they were dealing with the Holy as personal, and that in the relationship to that Holy, they, too were persons (1961, 232; 1969, 55–61). God is not identified with impersonal cosmic processes, nor is the human being dissolved into those processes. For Christians God is also understood as person-in-relationship, in the concept of the Trinity, in which each member is a person defined in relationship to the other persons.

(2) In the Hebrew–Christian tradition, God does not deal with us only impersonally through deterministic processes, or treat us as things, but rather carries on a history with us. In the unfolding of this history, it becomes apparent that we are valuable to God.

For Christians, this becomes most intensely real in the appearance of God in Jesus Christ, whose preaching and behavior underscored God's care for us as a community and as individuals. Our personhood is characterized as being created in the image of God, a matter that I will discuss at greater length.

(3) Humans are reinforced in their understanding of themselves as persons through their calling by God. The fact that their lives are a calling from God underscores that, however else they relate to the world, they relate to it as a gift and a calling extended to themselves by God. In this sense, the openness to the world that characterizes all living things, including humans, is a process that not only defines us, but also becomes an openness to God, whereby we actualize our personhood-in-vocation to the world and to God (see Pannenberg 1972).

(4) The most poignant aspect of our being-in-relationship is our life with others, with the Thou who calls forth our personhood and to whom we respond with the personhood, thus becoming both more deeply aware of our personhood and also fashioning it in relationship.

To say that our being persons is grounded in a network of relationships is thus elaborated in terms of relationship to the world itself, in its totality, to the Thou of other persons, individually and in community, and to the fullness of time, in the form of the world's future and our own future, which touches upon both our destiny and our calling. Or, in other terms, we are creatures who are formed by our openness to our world, which in turn becomes openness to God and to other persons, as well. In relationship and in openness to the world, we become persons.

The Imago Dei: Ground for the Possibility and the Necessity of the Human Person

All that I have said up to this point can be summarized and intensified in the theological concept of creation in the image of God. This concept has often been cited as the single most important statement that the Judeo–Christian–Muslim tradition makes concerning human beings. For Christians the image of God is instantiated normatively in Jesus. Although this assertion has had a long and rich tradition of interpretation, there is no consensus on exactly what it means; there is no single official or even standard interpretation of the concept of the image of God. In what follows, I will offer my own interpretation.

I start from the straightforward assumption that the image of God refers to that which portrays or sets forth God. To say that humans are the image of God means, therefore, that humans are somehow to be a portrayal or representation of God in the creation. Human beings were created, according to Christian faith, for this purpose. I am interpreting the concept of the image of God, therefore, to speak of the purpose of human being. Such an interpretation stands in sharp contrast to many past efforts that have in some way used the concept of the image of God to undergird the notion that humans are of greater value than the rest of nature, or that since they are superior to the rest of nature, they are destined to dominate it and exploit it for their own benefits.

The interpretation as dominator seems strange to me, although one can understand how exegesis of Genesis prompted it. I have images of loved ones in my home – a photo of my grandmother, my grandfather's gold pocket watch. What do those images do for me? They remind me of who my grandmother and grandfather were, and what they meant to me. They do not tell me that they were the best grandparents in the world, but rather carry the memory of their specific identities for me.

In analogy, our being created in the image of God carries a statement of our purpose, to set forth the presence of God in the world. This alternative view of being created in the image of God is expressed ritually for me in the prayers that we say in my congregation after we have received the bread and wine of the Holy Communion. We pray: 'Holy God, in this eucharist you reveal your faithfulness to us, your beloved children. Anoint us with your Spirit, that we may be for the world signs of your grace and compassion. Grant this through Christ our Lord.' We also pray during the offertory, 'With these gifts of bread and wine, we dedicate ourselves to the care and redemption of all that you have made.'

Interpreted in this way, creation in the image of God makes personhood possible, because it epitomizes the personal relationship that God has entered into with us and the calling that is given to us in that relationship. It also makes personhood necessary, because it is only as free, centered selves, that we can decide to carry out the kinds of behaviors that can serve to portray God to the creation, in the paradigm of Jesus Christ. Our possibilities for personhood are set in motion as we respond to the calling that is set before us.

What Memes Do:
A Closing Word on Methodology

In his essay on our topic, philosopher Philip Clayton writes:

> I am not convinced that direct battles between neurosciences and theology (or direct concordances for that matter) will stand up to closer analysis until a deeper mediation has been achieved. Instead, the neurosciences raise a question closer to home than disputes about God: the question of who *we* are. Progress in neuroscience challenges, or at least is often taken to challenge, cherished notions of what it is to be a human person: self-consciousness, soul, 'thinking being,' free will. Unless and until we manage to defend a notion of the person that preserves concepts such as these *in light of* what we now know about the human brain, language about God, and any work such language is supposed to do, will appear gratuitous. (2000, 1)

Clayton then proceeds to build a sophisticated philosophical edifice that can preserve the cherished notions of self that he mentions, culminating in what he calls a concept of 'emergentist supervenience.' I believe that I, too, have pursued the aim of preserving concepts of self and person that carry the freight of deep human concerns that have emerged in our Western history, and I have done so in light of what we know about the evolutionary history of *Homo sapiens* and its brain. However, I have taken quite a different path from the philosopher, and I have included generous amounts of God-language, taking the risk that it might indeed appear gratuitous. Let me for a moment comment on my method, in contrast to a more rigorous philosophical methodology like Clayton's.

The nub of my analysis has been the emergence of *Homo sapiens* as a cultural creature. To recall my earlier comments, culture consists of learned and taught patterns of behavior and the symbol systems that interpret and justify those behaviors. Culture, as psychologist Mihaly Csikszentmihalyi reminds us, depends for its functioning on effective *organization of the consciousness*. This is the central human issue of culture (Csikszentmihalyi 1987, 1991). This is another way of saying that the central issue is: What should guide us in the construction and conduct of our culture? The values we hold to, the world-views we live in, the decisions we make, all flow from the ways in which our consciousness is organized. In scientific terms, it is the psychological dimension of our personality that plays the role of gatekeeper between our genetic and cultural inputs, on the one hand, and what we shall select to pay most attention to and therefore act upon, on the other hand. This gatekeeper-function and decision-making rest on the foundation of how consciousness is organized. This gatekeeping function also offers a major opportunity for research by the neurosciences. What is the neurobiological component in this gatekeeping behavior?

The organization of consciousness takes place by constructing *memes* (the cultural counterpart to genes), which take our genetic evolution into account, but 'at the same time point to possibilities to which our biological inheritance is not yet sensitive' (Csikszentmihalyi, 1991; Csikszentmihalyi and Massimini 1985) These memes are deeply immersed in the particularities of our evolving world, but they focus upon what those particularities *can become*. This is the most important component for organizing our consciousness, our focus on what these very natural bodies and brains, in this most natural world, can become.

Roger Sperry, a Nobel laureate in brain research, gave expression to this insight when he said that the most powerful thing in the world is not the nuclear armaments of the nations, it is rather the *values* that inhabit the minds of those whose hands are on the switches that release those armaments. Those values, which image so concretely what the minds believe the world can become, are the centers of power. He might have said that the ways in which the consciousness of those minds is organized is the key factor, because it determines how the nuclear warheads will be employed.

Religion's Role in Human Evolution

Culture is where religion happens; religion is located within human culture. Religion has emerged within the cultural phase of evolution. What does religion do, what is it for, in the cultural realm? It is a primary force for the organization of consciousness and therefore for the world-views and values, and decisions that drive culture. Religion is above all concerned with what the natural world can become, its possibilities. Religion's adaptive success in strengthening individual psyches and mobilizing group spirit flows from its vision of what the world can become. You will note that with these words, I am accounting for the place of religion and its function in terms of evolution. This is an evolutionary interpretation of religion's function. I am, in other words, proceeding *in the light of* what we now know about human evolution, including the evolution of the brain.

In order to play its role, religion must generate the stories, rituals, and moral codes of meaning on the basis of its heritage, but in the currency of the present moment. To invoke the genetic metaphor, our genome is a heritage that we bring with us into the present, but the organism that carries that heritage will die unless it succcessfully negotiates a passage into the next generations – that is what the term 'inclusive fitness' is all about. Negotiating meaning in the present time – that is at the heart of religion's task. Or, we might say that organizing consciousness in *viable* ways for passage into the next generation is religion's contribution to human evolution.

The theological interpretations I have offered in this presentation, culminating in my interpretation of the *Imago Dei*, are meme proposals that I consider to be in touch with the Western tradition and specifically the contribution of Christian faith and theology. They are set forth as proposals for consideration. They propose that unless our understanding of ourselves as persons includes at least the concerns that I have set forth, in whatever rhetorical framework, secular humanistic, or according to the community traditions of the various world's religions, or Christian – unless we hold to these, the evolution of the human species will prove abortive, because the possibilities of what we have thus far become within the history of nature's evolution will go un-realized. With regard to what it means for humans to be persons, this is the discussion with which theology hopes to engage our culture today.

References

ASHBROOK, JAMES, and ALBRIGHT, CAROL. 1997. *The Humanizing Brain: Where Religion and Neuroscience Meet*, Cleveland: Pilgrim Press.

ATKINS, PETER. 1987. 'Purposeless People,' in A. Peacocke and G. Gillett (eds), *Persons and Personality: A Contemporary Inquiry*, Oxford: Basil Blackwell, 180–96.

BRUN, RUDOLF. 1994. 'Integrating Evolution: A Contribution to the Christian Doctrine of Evolution,' *Zygon* 29.3, 259–74.

——. 1999. 'Does God Play Dice? A Response to Niels Gregersen,' *Zygon* (forthcoming).

CLAYTON, PHILIP. 2000. 'Neuroscience, the Person, and God: An Emergent Account,' Notre Dame: The Vatican Observatory and the University of Notre Dame Press (forthcoming).

CRICK, FRANCIS. 1994. *The Astonishing Hypothesis: The Scientific Search for the Soul*, New York: Charles Scribner's Sons.

CSIKSZENTMIHALYI, MIHALY. 1987. 'On the Relationship Between Cultural Evolution and Human Welfare,' paper delivered to the American Association for the Advancement of Science, February 1987, Chicago.

——. 1991. 'Consciousness for the Twenty-First Century,' *Zygon* 26, 7–26.

—— and MASSIMINI, FAUSTO. 1985. 'On the Psychological Selection of Bio-Cultural Information,' *New Ideas in Psychology* 3, 115–38.

DANTO, ARTHUR. 1967. 'Persons,' in P. Edwards (ed.), *The Encyclopedia of Philosophy*, New York: Macmillan & Co.

D'AQUILI, EUGENE, and NEWBERG, ANDREW. 1993. 'Religious and Mystical States: A Neuropsychological Model,' *Zygon* 28, 177–200.

DEACON, TERRENCE. 1997. *The Symbolic Species: The Co-Evolution of Language and the Brain*, New York: W. W. Norton.

DENNETT, DANIEL. 1995. *Darwin's Dangerous Idea*, New York: Simon & Schuster.

EDELMAN, GERALD. 1992. *Bright Air, Brilliant Fire: On the Matter of the Mind*, New York: BasicBooks.

GAZZANIGA, MICHAEL. 1992. 'Nature's Mind: The Biological Roots of Thinking, Emotions,' in *Sexuality, Language, and Intelligence*, New York: BasicBooks.

GLASSMAN, ROBERT. 1996. 'Cognitive Theism: Sources of Accommodation Between Secularism and Religion,' *Zygon* 3, 157–207.

GREGERSEN, NIELS HENRIK. 1998. 'The Idea of Creation and the Theory of Autopoetic Processes,' *Zygon* 33, 333–67.

HEFNER, PHILIP. 1993. *The Human Factor: Evolution, Culture, Religion*, Minneapolis: Fortress Press.

KAUFFMAN, STUART. 1995. *At Home in the Universe: The Search for Laws of Self-Organization and Complexity*, New York: Oxford University Press.

KOLATA, GINA. 1998. 'Scientists Brace for Changes in Path of Human Evolution,' *The New York Times*, 12 March 1998, A1, A12.

MAYR, ERNST. 1988. *Toward a New Philosophy of Biology*, Cambridge, MA: Harvard University Press.

PANNENBERG, WOLFHART. 1961. 'Person,' in *Religion in Gechichte und Gegenwart*, vol. 5, 230–5. Tübingen: J. C. B Mohr (Paul Siebeck).

——. 1969. *Theology and the Kingdom of God*, Louisville: Westminster Press.

——. 1972. *What Is Man?*, Minneapolis: Fortress Press.

——. 1977. *Human Nature, Election, and History*, Louisville: Westminster Press.

SANFORD, NEVITT. 1968. 'Personality,' in D. Sills (ed.), *The International Encyclopedia of the Social Sciences*, vol. 11, 587, New York: Macmillan & Co.

SHARIF, MUZAFER. 1968. 'Selfhood,' in D. Sills (ed.), *The International Encyclopedia of the Social Sciences*, vol. 9, 151–9, New York: Macmillan & Co.

STRAWSON, P. F. 1959. *Individuals*, New York: Methuen.

TESKE, JOHN. 1996. 'The Spiritual Limits of Neuropsychological Life,' *Zygon* 31, 209–34.

THATCHER, ADRIAN. 1987. 'Christian Theism and the Concept of a Person,' in A. Peacocke and G. Gillett (eds), *Persons and Personality: A Contemporary Inquiry*, Oxford: Basil Blackwell, 180–96.

TILLICH, PAUL. 1948. *The Protestant Era*, Chicago: University of Chicago Press.

———. 1963. *Systematic Theology*, vol. 3, Chicago: University of Chicago Press.

———. 1988. *The Spiritual Situation in Our Technical Society*, Macon: Mercer University Press.

WALDROP, M. MITCHELL. 1992. *Complexity: The Emerging Science at the Edge of Chaos*, New York: Simon & Schuster.

WIGGINS, DAVID. 1987. 'The Person as Object of Science, as Subject of Experience, and as Locus of Value,' in A. Peacocke and G. Gillett (eds), *Persons and Personality: A Contemporary Inquiry*, Oxford: Basil Blackwell, 56–74.

WILSON, E. O. 1990. 'Biology and the Social Sciences,' *Zygon* 29, 71f.

6

Is the Autonomous Person of European Modernity a Sustainable Model of Human Personhood?

MICHAEL WELKER

I would like to present for discussion reflections on the concept of the person that combine ideas from philosophy, theology, and cultural sciences. I begin with a classic pre-modern concept of the person, namely 'the mask'. With the help of this concept I elaborate difficulties that we have today – that is, in late modernity or in so-called post-modernity – in developing a persuasive concept of the person that connects innerpersonal subjectivity and the public person. In Part II I describe the concept of the 'autonomous person' of modernity. I shall show that the autonomous person of modernity attained a high anthropological level in serving this task, and I shall explore the question of whether the autonomous person of European modernity can be regarded as a sustainable model of human personhood. In Part III I ask whether Christian theology both past and present can with good reason claim that the person is constituted not by autonomy, but by faith.[1] I shall

---

[1] Today, many persons prefer the term 'spirituality'. I will propose an understanding of faith which serves the intentions to address the emotional, affective and practical dimensions of piety, without losing the concentrated and cognitive aspects of the individual and communal relation to God.

show that in the modern period a reductionist theology and piety with highly abstract concepts of faith and of the 'God-human relation' has systematically obscured both the theological and the anthropological dimension of the person. In closing I shall consider the conditions under which the theological assertion that faith constitutes the person could be persuasive.

My presentation will suggest that the anthropological search for a concept of the person should take place in connection with work on theological questions. The search for a materially appropriate and complex concept of the person is supremely well suited to test the cooperation of natural sciences, humanities, and theology or theologically schooled religious studies.

I. A Pre-Modern Concept of the Person and the Difficulties It Reveals in Developing a Complex Understanding of the Person Today

Most dictionaries and other reference books state under the entry 'person' that the Greek word *prósopon* (face) and the Latin word *persona* refer to the *mask* through which an actor speaks. The expression can also signify the actor who wears the mask, and the role played by the actor. The expression thus intends a connection between the concrete individual (the actor), the typification on the basis of the role (through the mask), and the condition of being adjusted and attuned to a public spectrum of expectations (the role and its performance). However, modern thought seems to find it difficult to *understand* this pre-modern connection as 'person' and the person as this complex interface. In general, modern common sense seems to mix up the person, the individual, the singularity of the body, the subject, the self, the 'I', and other phenomena and concepts. It seems to have difficulties in differentiating and clearly relating the subjectivity behind the mask and the public, objective and objectified person in front of the mask.

Like the concept of 'person', most of these key anthropological concepts (the individual, the I, the subject) *mediate between the individual as a 'unique one' and the individual as 'an example or representative of the species'*. The polarity between, on the one hand, human singularity and uniqueness and, on the other hand, abstract human equality, as well as the mediation between these two poles, are obviously of the utmost importance to modern mentalities. The person represents such a mediation. This mediation is complex. It has to operate, so to speak, both in front of the mask and behind the mask. On the one hand, the person mediates human uniqueness and abstract equality objectively and for the outside world, for the surroundings of the individual: the objective and public self. On the other hand, the person links individual uniqueness and equality subjectively and for the inside. This inner, subjective mediation of singularity and equality brings about the differentiation and connection of the 'I' and the self – a mediation that we attribute to *subjectivity*. George Herbert Mead, Erik Erikson and others differentiated the 'I' and the self as subject and object of self-consciousness. A long anthropological debate, which is not yet consolidated, has reversed this relation and sees the self as the totality of 'states, qualities and actions' of a human individual, whose unity is actualized moment by moment in the 'I' (Pannenberg 1983, 214 ff.).

The individual person is the connection between the person's intimate self-reference, the person's external self-presentation, and the interrelations of a person's environment to her or his self-reference and self-presentation (the public self). Or, to operate with the pre-modern image: the individual person differentiates and relates the processes 'in front of the mask' and those 'behind the mask'. Via the person, via the mask, the individual mediates to the outside world uniqueness and equality, non-disposability and security of expectations. With regard to the mask from the inside, a person mediates and differentiates himself and his perception and stylization of himself. The person, visualized by the mask, is the interface both determined by and turned towards the outside world, and determined by and turned towards the inside. Through the person a human being adjusts and attunes herself both consciously and unconsciously in accordance with broad spectra of expecta-tions directed towards the person.

We adapt to a certain spectrum of fixed expectations, role stereotypes, and habits; we influence other spectra in the direction of change; and we avoid a third group of expectations altogether. In this process of grasping, presenting and forming ourselves we are 'a person'. In this process we prove to be individually unique *and* individually typical; we prove our subjectivity to be a unique *and* a general phenomenon.

By way of the personal mask – that is, the connection of uniqueness and security of expectations directed towards the outside world and towards the inside – a human being can refer in a definite way to the image of himself, which is not only self-made, but also created in social interaction. The individual can (to a certain degree) transform the mask – that is, the forms of appearance, action and reaction typical of his public self. The individual can thus influence the spectrum of fixed expectations that are directed towards the person in a manner that seems to go without saying. The person can, of course, also have the mask transformed from the outside. Or she can perceive the changes made without her explicit knowledge, and can and will try to adjust and attune herself to the different spectra of expectations in a new way.

In the same process, the human being certainly must both differentiate and relate the 'I' and the self behind the mask, so to speak, and develop her subjectivity. It is very difficult to grasp the interconnection of the processes behind and in front of the mask, the interconnection of the subjectivity, on the one hand, and the public and externally objectivized self, on the other. Indeed, just the processes that take place *in front of* the mask and with reference to it are very complex and difficult to grasp. The more the social environments become incalculable, the faster they change, the more difficult the integration of the person becomes. But if the culture and the individual fail to achieve this integration, the idea of the free person becomes nothing but an empty phrase.

As we have seen, the person integrates numerous problems and processes of adjustment and attunement that become blurred if we mix up person, individual, subjectivity, the 'I', etc. This confusion on the part of common sense provokes a welter of different one-sided and reductionist conceptions of personhood that partly even conflict with each other, although they seem to speak of the same matter. Very different elements of personhood or constellations of those elements can be grasped as *the* person. A number of one-sided forms can be passed off as 'the person', or can even be made to be the criterion for 'the person', such as an unsteady and bizarre individuality following his inclinations (the 'post-modern individual'), a subjectivity which gives security of expectations but is socially quite unadapted (the Bogart type), an abstract 'I' seeking to become his own self (the identity-search figure), a self turning with the change of public moral pressures (the typical petty-bourgeois individual), or a personality who controls the social environment with a strong sense for resonance (the success-type in market societies), to name only a few forms.

Several philosophers like Amélie Oksenberg Rorty (1998, 31 ff.) have drawn attention to the fact that with different social and cultural contexts, the definition of 'person' and of the essence of personhood changes. If we consider conceptions of the person that predominate in contemporary Western cultures, it seems to me that the intellectual understanding of the person still concentrates on what is going on *behind the mask, obviously in an ongoing reaction to the unintelligibility and complexity of what in our day and social environments takes place in front of the mask.* Most of what modern consciousness holds to be holy about the person seems to lie behind the mask: self-reference and familiarity with one's own self; the ability to refuse demands from the outside world, to say 'no' and to be self-determining; the free subjectivity in her differentiated adjustment and attunement of the 'I' and the self; the free cultivation of individual capabilities in the process of education based on one's own power and authority.

This process that we might term the *'subjectification of the person'* seems still to be in full swing in our cultures. This process did not seem to be problematic as long as it took place in environments whose communicative structures were dense and closely connected, and as long as it was directed against powerful, stable and stratified public institutions and hierarchical forms of organization and order. Quite the contrary, this process led to a strengthening of individuals and to a vivification of culture. The one-sided concentration on the processes behind the mask made sense as long as the conditions existing in front of the mask and with respect to it were densely ordered and relatively clearly definable. The strong counter-movements to the stable public institutions and hierarchies produced common aims and common forms – that is, stability – in modern subjectivity. Many forms of unity emerged time and again in the manifold processes of subjectification, because these processes reacted against the same environments, or against analogous, relatively stable environments. The individual variety of subjective self-references and the common belief in the person as a representative of the species were compatible. The communicative density of small or at least clear public contexts guaranteed the constant adjustment and attunement of individual one-sidedness and subjective arbitrariness to public expectations and realms of resonance.

The problems attendant upon this withdrawal 'behind the mask' become obvious as soon as the strong hierarchical public institutions are substituted by market-type configurations and media-stimulated pluralistic developments. The negative consequences of the modern withdrawal behind the mask indeed become recognizable as soon as human beings have to act in thinly structured or relatively diffuse public environments. Earlier than anybody else, some North American cultural critics grasped these displacements with terms such as 'the minimal self' (Lash 1984; Oksenberg Rorty 1988, 31 ff.), 'the culture of narcissism' (Lash 1979), 'the decay and end of public life', 'the tyranny of intimacy' (Sennett 1974), etc.

If we read the cultural dynamics of contemporary Western societies correctly, there is an unbroken fascination with the radical uniqueness of the individual in our societies. At the same time, in late modernity the abstract individualism of modernity becomes challenged in several ways. It is not without reason that nowadays competitive sports and electronic popular music are the forms in which individuals can become 'public persons' with an extra large realm of resonance. The public persons in competitive sports and entertainment music mirror the way in which current societies search and long for 'the person'. Modern culture provoked the subjectification of the person, the withdrawal behind the mask. It thus aimed at the maximum increase in concrete individuality.

What late modern cultures see, is that the maximum increase in concrete individuality is provided by the *single body* and by *individual feeling*. Now the single body and individual feeling have to be presented *in front of* the mask in a way that shows that this unique individual is to the highest degree also typical and able to function as a representative of the species in a way that finds immediate resonance. Without any doubt, we find successful syntheses with regard to such a public objectification of the body in competitive sports, and with regard to the communication of emotionality in electronic popular music. If the latent cultural parameters remain what they are at the moment, there will be no diminution in the power of these one-sided and even distortive forms of centring on the person, which through their presentation via the mass media are surrounded with an aura that is nothing short of religious. On the basis of our findings it is, by the way, not difficult to predict that pornography will continue to experience a boom as a side-effect of the helpless search for the person with emphasis on the publication of both individual corporeality and individual feeling.

If we want to change this state of affairs it first is important to understand what help the modern concept of the autonomous person offered in mediating between the processes behind the mask and those in front of the mask. It is important to examine whether the modern concept of the autonomous person can be a paradigm of personhood as such.

II. Why the Autonomous Person of European Modernity Can Seem to Be a Paradigm of Personhood, and Why It Cannot Provide a Sustainable Model

The tremendous integrative power of the modern concept of the autonomous person became clear to me at a conference of the Heidelberg International Wissenschaftsforum in the summer of 1997. We had brought together philosophers, psychologists, ethnologists and other scholars in the humanities from all over the world to consider the question of whether the concept of the autonomous person can also be found in non-European cultures.

Sinologists, Egyptologists, Indologians and Hellenists, as well as ethnologists who study contemporary cultures, put forward various candidates for the concept of autonomy, but the discussions showed that none of them measured up to the modern concept of autonomy. If autonomy is understood merely as autarchy, we find it present over 4000 years ago in Egypt (Jan Assmann). In the sixth century BC a concept of the soul (*atman*) was developed in India that focuses on a self that can be influenced only by itself (Klaus Butzenberger). Also an agile life in an abundance of roles and perspectives on oneself, engaging in mere resistance to heteronomy and to all varieties of being incorporated from the outside, does not measure up to the level of modern autonomy – although it represents a form that might appear as 'autonomy' to so-called postmodern mentalities. This shifting and evasive identity, which I have termed autoplexy, is found not only among the yuppies of late modernity, but also, for example, in contemporary African tribal cultures (John and Jean Comaroff). An important basic characteristic of the European conception of the autonomous person is already found in the agonal self in classical Greece. Through permanent competitive self-assertion, this form of the self argues for regarding competition as a basic form of cultural formation (Egon Flaig).

But the modern European concept of the autonomous person is built upon several further differentiations. Using rabbinic interpretations of Old Testament traditions, Michael Fishbane called attention to an important differentiation that casts light on the constellations both behind and in front of the mask. In those rabbinic interpretations, one candidate for the 'autonomous person' is the *religiously distinguished self, purified and immunized against external influences. The other candidate is the individual performer of a religiously coded moral activity.* As we shall see, both perspectives – on the one hand, a pure self immune to alien determinations (type: Noah, who 'walked with God'), and on the other hand, a normative shaper of culture, society and the world (type: Abraham, who 'walked before God') – are bound together, in secularized form, in the modern European concept of the autonomous person.

The modern autonomous person seeks to structure and shape the field in front of the mask by engaging in a continual struggle with himself behind the mask. The autonomous person of modernity must continually regain the unity of the person. At the most basic level, the autonomous person of modernity must *continually regain the unity and constancy of the person* by, on the one hand, striving for *coherence in rule-governed self-direction* and, on the other hand, *dominating one's own corporeal, sensual nature*. The 'agonal self' is thus interiorized and verifies autonomy in an enduring battle with itself and in a continuous process of triumphing over self. According to the modern Credo, this continually renewed self-acquisition goes hand in hand with a moral self-presentation that commands respect and with a continual process of exercising rational and moral influence on one's social surroundings. The operations behind the mask receive their compensation in front of the mask, so to speak. Autonomy has a dynamically exemplary effect on other human beings, inasmuch as it summons them to become increasingly steady and increasingly perfected selves. In theory at any rate, this reciprocal process is supposed to lead to a steady increase in the moral and rational coherence of the entire community.

The most striking conception of the autonomous person, and the one which probably has most influenced cultural history, is to be found in the moral philosophy of Immanuel Kant. According to the well-known teaching of this moral philosophy, the person acquires and verifies his autonomy:

(1) not only by bringing sensual drives under subjective rules, but also by examining these rules to see whether they correspond to the universal law of reason;

(2) by reforming the rules for his own action in accordance with the universal law of reason.

When Kant published his *Critique of Practical Reason* he was convinced that this concept of the autonomous person would quickly take hold of mentalities and become effective both theoretically and practically. In Kant's view, a consciousness of dignity, of self-respect and of freedom accompanies the experience of the autonomy of moral reason, and this consciousness will become ever stronger, eventually attaining dominance both in individual human beings and in relations between human beings. Yet in spite of the great success of his moral philosophy, Kant soon saw himself confronted with the following dilemma: the prospect of a steady progress in the dominance of reason over sensual drives was by no means clear, either in the individual course of life or in public morality. Kant had evidently overestimated the power of reason. At the same time he had underestimated the power of sensual drives. This led to the sceptical response that wondered whether it was a mere illusion to think that reason could achieve dominance in a sensually determined being (Welker 1975).

As is well known, in his later years Kant reacted to this problem by turning again to religion. In his *Religion Within the Limits of Reason Alone* he invents a metaphysical history of the Fall. The Fall consists in the fact that human beings set up a false ordering in the relation between reason and sensuality. Because they subordinate reason to sensuality, because they confuse freedom with the condition of being driven by the senses, reason must gain itself a hearing by appearing as an 'ought'. Human beings must be brought to freedom by compulsion. And religion can, as Kant says, help by serving as a 'vehicle' of morality in this arduous process of the forming the autonomous person.

In spite of the enduring success story of this concept of the autonomous person, today we have a fairly clear picture of the weaknesses and deficiencies that, already in Kant's work, displaced this concept from its status as a supposed fact to its status as an – even problematic – ideal. Kant's negative depiction of sensuality, and the attendant inability to do justice both to the concrete, unique human individual and to real, complex relations in social life, were seen early on as a problem. The intellectual development of Friedrich Schleiermacher, the most significant theologian of the nineteenth century, occurred in a continual effort to correct these weaknesses of the modern concept of the autonomous person (Welker 1999).

Yet the *modern understanding of autonomy not only fails to grasp the authenticity of the unique corporeal and sensual person. It also under-*

estimates the contextuality of morality and the mutability of rationality.
Fixed on the disembodied person primarily behind the mask, fixed
on abstract subjectivity and its moral powers of influence, the
modern concept of the autonomous person cannot assign any
clearly definable place to the way in which human beings are
shaped by modernity's social and cultural processes of differentiation. The modern concepts of morality and rationality were
unable to prevent entire societies that appealed to these governing
powers from being possessed by chauvinist, fascist, racist and
ecologically brutal mentalities. Moreover, the modern concept of
the autonomous person has extreme difficulty maintaining its
claims to orientation and universality, because it seems unable
either to coordinate the rationalities and moralities of the differentiated subsystems (media, economy, law, education, politics,
religion, science), or to limit their powers of self-assertion.

Insight into the limitations of what can be achieved by the
modern concept of the autonomous person does not automatically
suggest that we should turn to a religious and theological understanding of the person. But a circumspect consideration of its
limitations does direct us again and again to themes that are
familiar from the history of theology: the relation between the
'outer' and the 'inner' human being; the relations between body,
consciousness, and the somewhat nebulous entities 'spirit' and
'soul' (or perhaps entities that have *become* nebulous); faith in the
care extended by the God who deserves to be called 'Creator of the
world' to the concrete, individual human being; God's engagement
with the sin that can completely possess and corrupt our moralities
and rationalities; and so on. Yet it is not triumphalistically, but
cautiously, even sceptically that I turn to the theological thesis:
Faith constitutes the person. Does faith or spirituality indeed
constitute the person?

III. Why Can Christian Theology Claim that Faith Constitutes the Person?

The popular understanding of 'faith' in contemporary Western
societies is that a believing individual is utterly certain of something

'wholly Other', of a 'transcendent' power, agent, or vaguely conceived Person, that at the same time, however, is intimately near. Since the 'Beyond', the 'ultimate point of reference of creaturely dependence' is included in this utmost certainty that is then called 'faith', this relation of dependence approximates an emphatic self-reference. The great Swiss theologian Karl Barth was right when he described it as an 'indirect Cartesianism': I feel somehow dependent, therefore I am.

This conception of 'faith' approaches and even collapses into emphatic self-reference. Thus religious communication – in order to distinguish religious and non-religious experience of this inner certainty and feeling of otherness – has regularly thematized this 'faith' while stigmatizing all forms of self-reference. To the same degree that the inner certainty – understood as 'faith' – was treasured, all forms of self-reference were denounced as 'sin'. Any attempt to distinguish between innocent, trivial, healthy, distortive and even demonic forms of self-reference seemed risky. A paradoxical and neuroticizing mentality captured this religious form, since it proved extremely difficult, indeed impossible, to distinguish this empty certainty from a very simple and basic form of human self-reference that had come to terms with its inner structure: namely, that all self-reference has to include some element of difference if it wants to experience 'certainty'. The upside of this seemed to be that nobody could escape this type of 'faith' – at least not in cultures and among mentalities that are based on the self-reference of the individual, which is to say, cultures that belong to the 'modern world-society'.

Seen from the outside, this impoverished form called 'faith' contains in itself the elements of immediacy and negation, intimate self-awareness and the experience of difference. Since this can appear both as a religious form and as a basic form of dialectical self-reflexivity (unity of unity and difference), it can be interpreted as the 'feeling of the utmost dependence' (Schleiermacher), as the simultaneity of self-assurance and self-challenge in the encounter with the 'Thou shalt' of the moral law (Kant), as the unity and tension of 'essence and existence' (Tillich), and in multifarious other ways, both religious and non-religious, depending on the communicative context in which it occurs. From Schleiermacher and Kierkegaard to Bultmann and Gordon Kaufman there have been many theological endeavours to come to terms with this type of empty 'faith'. Most of them have in common that they want to demonstrate that this utmost certainty, on the one hand, is clearly an anthropological phenomenon while, on the other hand, it is seen as God-given, as sponsored by grace and not a trivial event or the result of an everyday perceptual enterprise.

This experience of immediacy and negation, of a religious certainty called 'faith', could seem to be extremely precious. It seems to allow us to introduce religious communication at practically any point. Nobody can escape this experience of immediacy and negation. As soon as a person tries to thematize her 'inner self' she runs into this religious certainty. What is the element of 'otherness' I encounter when I reach the utmost depth of my inner self? Is this God? In a form that appeals to the modern mind, we seem to have at hand what Calvin called the 'natural awareness', the presentiment of the Divine. But it is a culturally tamed and domesticated natural awareness. Where Calvin saw a vague awe in the face of aesthetic powers, cosmic laws, and social orders, the modern religious variant has only this arid notion of dialectical self-awareness.

Vast regions of theology, of teaching and of proclamation in the classic mainline churches have treasured this form of abstract and empty 'faith' very highly. They have done much to shield this empty certainty from the discovery of religious arbitrariness, availability and ambivalence. They bought into the idealist assertion that this certainty was the 'ground' of self-consciousness, the key to all epistemological and moral worth, and the very foundation of personhood. They clothed this poor form with abundant variants of the rhetoric of 'wholeness'. And they tried to reinforce the differentiation between a self-reference given by the divine and a self-reference taken or performed in the secular world. However, this differentiation could not be reinforced on the basis of the underlying theoretical construction. As the vast debates on the reflection theory of self-consciousness teach us, there is nothing but an arbitrary distinction between the predominance of the 'active' side and the predominance of the 'passive' side in this basic dialectical experience. Both aspects co-emerge in the experience of self-referential activity. The often heated debate over the question of what would and should be the true and 'faithful' order of giving and receiving, of activity and passivity in the relation of God and the human being was like a fight over the question of whether 'the emperor's new clothes' were black or white.

This analysis of the inner texture of a typically modern type of 'faith', however, should not lead us to underestimate its power. This form of faith allows us to fuse religious and secular mentalities. It allows us to fuse religious and moral communication. Above all, it is an excellent focus for a culture that tries to trigger the greed-fulfilment mechanism as perfectly as possible: already but not yet, not yet but already; intimacy with myself and the encounter with otherness; utmost certainty and dialectical difference. Yet this type of faith allows for a religious coding of universalist mentalities. And it seems recursively to bless religious mentalities with a universalist aura. It continuously signals the message 'In a latent way, a reasonable person cannot but be religious!'

Like Calvin, who emphasized the power of the 'natural aware-ness' of the Divine – despite its vagueness, ambiguity and ambivalence – we should acknowledge the power of the modern notion of 'faith' just described. We should acknowledge its power, but we should also clearly indicate that it blocks and blurs a clear concept of the person and a convincing understanding of God. Having examined pre-modern and modern forms of personhood and having addressed difficulties the contemporary world has with the concept of the person, we can clearly see that theology has to do much better than promoting the reductionist understanding of faith just described. It is the task of theology to help explore the relation between God and the human person without reducing both sides to mere reference points.[2]

We turn to this task if we take as our starting point not the vacuous modern understanding of faith, but Luther's or Paul's understanding of faith. Here we find a way of talking about faith

---

[2] Without driving God behind the mask, too!

in which the subjective relationship with God is always connected with objective faith, included in it, supported by it, and nourished by it. We find the subjective relationship with God always bound into a dynamic structure of persuasion traversed by certainties that have been tested in diverse ways, and by diverse quests for truth. *This dynamic structure of persuasion functions as a medium of communication.* Human beings can gain access to this medium, whether the position from which they are coming be one of uncertainty, of distance from faith, of lack of faith, or of enmity towards faith. In contrast to other communication media oriented towards truth (e.g. mathematics), faith in God is highly sensitive and open to the concrete individual and his emotional and affective forms of experience. 'Faith' is thus also understood as that individual or shared access to the dynamic structure of persuasion with regard to the living God which both strengthens and is strengthened by this dynamic structure. When human beings believe in God, they gain access to the medium of faith, they enter into this dynamic structure of persuasion. The attendant problems of not confusing God and faith must not provoke us to construct a God without faith: for instance, as an empty point of reference of indeterminate individual certainty or of arbitrary private convictions. Luther was right when he saw that 'God and faith belong together'.

If we recognize that faith is constituted in this way, we can abandon false dichotomies such as 'faith and knowledge'. Since faith relates to the living God, and since it is open not only to the rational and cognitive experiences of human beings, but also to their emotional and affective experiences, it is so to speak softer, more open to revision than is knowledge. But it is most definitely accompanied and permeated by knowledge. This knowledge of faith, shared consciously by many persons and unconsciously by many others, evinces astounding continuities and regularities – even in comparison with the knowledge of the natural sciences. The modern emptying out of faith's contents has in part driven the knowledge of faith out of public consciousness, so now this knowledge must be reactivated if we wish to grasp and to describe such complex phenomena as that of the person. In relating to the individual person by means of faith, God not only accepts and takes seriously the individual human being in her spiritual, corporeal, sensual and emotional uniqueness. In faith God also gives this human being a universal worth. For Christians this worth consists in their becoming one person with Christ, as Luther says. They become bearers of God's presence on earth.

It would be fascinating to investigate how this worth of the human being is grounded and brought to expression in other religions.[3] In any case we already see the first basic features of how the constitution of the person by faith brings with it a very complex concept of the person. On the one hand, the depth of the concrete, unique person can be taken seriously and must not be reduced to abstract subjectivity. On the other hand, the universal worth of the person is taken seriously, since in faith the person is ordained to be a bearer of God's presence on this earth. After we have seen that this God can indeed be reduced to an abstract entity inhabiting the 'beyond', to an 'ultimate point of reference', or to similar religious inventions, and after we have seen that this leads to faith becoming vacuous and to the sought after concept of the person becoming fuzzy or simply being lost, we will be somewhat more careful in how we handle the knowledge of faith. Within the Christian churches we shall have to ask what it means to become one with the person of Christ, with the Risen One who reveals himself in his post-Easter body with his various members and gifts. In conversation with non-Christian religions and with secular attitudes we shall have to pursue the question of what it means to be the image of the creative God when we do not go along with the modern reductionism and the systematic drive towards religious vacuity. But in both contexts we need self-critical and critical conversation with philosophy, the humanities and the natural sciences, if we wish to prove that a theological orientation is helpful in the effort to attain an understanding of the person that is adequate to its object.

Without dragging you too deeply into technical theological questions, I have at least attempted in a fourfold way to call your

---

[3] And, of course, how secular and agnostic mentalities describe the individual and common approbation of human dignity and worth.

attention to what a theological perspective with an interdisciplinary orientation can introduce into this discussion:

(1) The uninhibited recourse to insights and concepts that lie far back in world history, and that we cannot take over directly, but from whose sensitivity to truth and reality we can learn (the mask, the person constituted by faith).

(2) The reconstruction of efforts at knowledge in popular cultural developments, from which highbrow social and intellectual discussion tends to keep its distance (the fixed concentration on heros and heroines of entertainment music and of competitive sports as a plausible, albeit misguided search for the paradigm of personhood).

(3) The critical and self-critical engagement with philosophically and religiously honed, extremely successful cultural forms (modern autonomy and vacuous faith as immediate relationship to that which is 'wholly other').

(4) Most important, though, is the perspective that I was only able to sketch within the framework of our theme: by relating the interdisciplinary questions to the living God, theology can open up new terrain for cultural and historical learning, if theology does not close itself off to the questions of certainty and truth posed by the other sciences, and if theology does not attempt to promulgate totalitarian religious thought. The constitution of the person by faith addresses not only the richness of the individual, its rational and emotional dimensions, its cognition and its modes of living. It also leads behind the mask and it structures the realm in front of the mask. It is God the creator who constitutes the complex unity of the person and the complex interdependence of the creatures. Without addressing God's creative activity, appreciated by faith, we do not gain a perspective on the unity of the public person and the unity of creation.

This does not mean that God relates to everything and that God connects everything with everything as totalitarian religious thought sees it. Totalitarian religious thought simply relates everything – in fact in a thoughtless manner – to God. God is the 'ground of all being', the 'all-determining reality', the 'cause of everything' – so run the corresponding ciphers and jargon phrases. Totalitarian religious thought remains undeterred by everything from the ironic queries as to whether God also created my pants button and willed the staggering steps of the drunk, to the very serious questions of theodicy. Totalitarian religious thought simply relates all and everything to God and God to all and everything – and thereby leaves faith and theology behind. It is by no means easy to make clear that totalitarian religious thought suppresses or stultifies faith and theology. Faith certainly sees the possibility that every event *could* in principle be related to God. But faith's interest in God, in the knowledge of God, and in the knowledge of reality in the light of the knowledge of God leads faith to ask where that relationship becomes *clear*. In totalitarian religious thought's vague assurance that everything is somehow or other related to God, *nothing becomes clear*. In my view, the great opportunity provided by interdisciplinary collaboration on a materially appropriate concept of the person is that we will render both totalitarian religious thought and a tired agnosticism equally superfluous by the shared search for understanding and by the quest for the truth that illuminates and liberates both faith and knowledge.

What have we gained concretely with regard to the search for a model for human personhood?

The modern concept of the autonomous person has greatly distanced us from the corporeal, sensual person and from the culturally and socially conditioned person. It has contributed to idealist philosophy reigning for a while as queen of the sciences and humanities. But it has been unable to satisfy the high expectations it awakened. At the same time we need to value the major feat of integration that the concept of the modern autonomous person has accomplished with regard to many concepts of personhood and freedom. When it comes to consistency, this integration is simply superior to that of most pre-modern and postmodern proposals. The autonomous person of modernity poses itself the problem of how to mediate between the subjectivity behind the mask and the public person in front of the mask. Its answer is: by fighting against the sensual condition of the person and by shaping the moral communication. This answer has lost its convincing power. But this does not mean that the assertion that faith constitutes the person will find open ears, without further ado.

In the modern period, the theological concept of the person constituted by faith not only has fallen victim to philosophical reductionism, but has also been completely emptied of content spiritually. Therefore the abstract God–human relation, which combines two points of reference by means of a primitive relation of unequal powers, must be replaced by a materially appropriate description of the relation between the living creative God and the human person in the midst of creaturely existence. We have tried to unfold the notion of the person with the help of the pre-modern notion of the mask. We thus saw the need and the difficulty, to relate the subjectivity behind the mask to the public self in front of the mask. We saw the need to do this in a different way than fighting and denouncing the sensual self. We also saw the difficulties to gain a notion of the unity of the public self without losing the richness of the concrete person and its complex environments. Here the relation of the living and creative God to the human person, encountered and disclosed by faith becomes a very attractive focus to explore the unity of the public person and its relation to the sensual, bodily self. To work on this description is the task of theology, which must free itself from subordination to a reductionist philosophy. But to work on this description is also the task of the sciences that wish to hold themselves critically accountable to the classical religious and philosophical standards for a complex concept of the person. If we ask for the unity of the public person, the unity in front of the mask, and if we explore its relation to the concrete subjectivity in the fullness of its cognitive and emotional, theoretical and practical striving behind the mask, we cannot escape the religious dimensions of human life and personhood.

References

CALVIN, J. 1957. *Institutes of the Christian Religion*, I. 3–5, trans. H. Beveridge, vol. 1, Grand Rapids, Mich.: Eerdmans.

LASH, CH. 1979. *The Culture of Narcissism: American Life in an Age of Diminishing Expectations*, New York and London: Norton.

——. 1984. *The Minimal Self: Psychic Survival in Troubled Times*, New York and London: Norton.

LUTHER, M. WA 40/I on Gal. 2:20.

OKSENBERG RORTY, A. 1988. *Mind in Action: Essays in the Philosophy of Mind*, Boston: Beacon.

PANNENBERG, WOLFHART. 1983. *Anthropologie in theologischer Perspektive*, Göttingen: Vandenhoeck.

SENNET, R. 1974. *The Fall of Public Man*, Cambridge: Cambridge University Press.

WELKER, M. 1975. *Der Vorgang Autonomie: Philosophische Beiträge zur Einsicht in theologischer Rezeption und Kritik*, Neukirchen: Neukirchener.

——. 1998. *Creation and Reality*, Minneapolis: Fortress.

——. 1999. 'We Live Deeper Than We Think': The Genius of Schleiermacher's Earliest Ethics, *Theology Today* 56, 1999, 169–79.

PART II:
SUPERVENIENCE, MIND
AND CULTURE

7

The Peril and Promise of Supervenience for the Science–Theology Discussion

DENNIS BIELFELDT

I. Introduction

A central problem in the science–theology discussion is the question of how divine action is possible in a *causally closed* physical universe. How can it be that God acts within nature, when each and every event in nature is caused by, and causes, other events within nature? This principle is clearly displayed where e is a natural event, and C the causal operation:

$$< \left\{ e_1, e_2, e_3 \dots e_n \right\}, C >$$

Natural science assumes that the set of physical events is *closed* under causality because it presupposes that the event which results from causally operating upon any member of that set is itself a member of that set.

While the problem of causal closure remains problematic for advocates of divine agency, other features of twentieth-century science are clearly more congenial to divine action than were corresponding notions within the Newtonian paradigm. For instance, while the older paradigm interpreted natural change to be merely a rearrangement of fixed components, the present scientific context understands it to involve genuine *emergence*. Furthermore, in much of contemporary science chance and unpredictability have super-seded global determinism, relationality has replaced atomism, holism has supplanted reductionism, and multi-level approaches to reality have succeeded dualistic ones (Barbour 1990, 218 ff.). Many believe that this new scientific context is fully compatible with belief in a divine agent actually *acting* in the universe.

Central to the new scientific paradigm is the notion of 'hier-archies of complexity' (Ellis and Murphy 1996, 22ff.). The idea is simple. Physics is the fundamental science referring to the most basic entities (quarks, hadrons, or whatever) and their physical properties (spin, charm, or whatever). In ascending to higher levels, however, we discover entities constituted by entities at lower levels, but having sets of properties distinctive to their particular level. For instance, the chemical properties emerging at a higher level are different from, and *irreducible* to, the physical properties of spin and charm. Likewise biological properties are irreducible to chemical properties, and psychological properties to biological ones.[1]

Recently, the term 'supervenience' has been popping up in the science–theology discussion in regard to the question of the relation of levels, and the associated question of the possibility of divine agency.[2] For instance, in *On the Moral Nature of the Universe*, Nancey Murphy and George Ellis use supervenience to speak of the relation

---

[1] The precise nature of the supposed irreducibility of the emergents is a matter of considerable philosophical interest. Teller (1992) distinguishes three types of emergent properties: (1) relational properties of the whole; (2) non-relational properties of the whole which *do not* supervene upon the non-relational properties of the parts; and (3) non-relational properties of a whole which *do* supervene upon the non-relational properties of the parts. While (3) is thought to be the paradigmatic case of supervenience, Teller argues convincingly that supposed cases of (3) are actually cases of (1). The upshot of this is that the putative failure of reducibility characteristic of emergence is due to the fact that the properties of the whole are related 'to other properties "external" to the whole in question' (152). If Teller is correct, then prospects for genuine emergence are bleak indeed.

[2] While this is not the place to give the various definitions of supervenience, David Lewis provides the central idea: 'we have supervenience when there could be no difference of one sort without differences of another sort' (1986, 14).

of constitution and irreducibility between properties of levels. A mental event supervenes on a brain state if the former is constituted by the latter without being reduced to it, and if the two are non-identical (Ellis and Murphy 1996, 34). Murphy and Ellis carefully point out that such a notion of supervenience is entirely consistent with the notion of a *top-down effect*: a *boundary condition* established at a higher level can influence the course of events at a lower level, e.g. the position of a macrolevel piston changes the local motion of microlevel molecules in the gas (Ellis and Murphy 1996, 28). After suggesting that human agency uses determinate top-down effects in the expression of its freedom, they claim that upper-level 'philosophical thought patterns and understandings ... have a force of their own that shapes what happens at the physical level through *top-down action*' (Ellis and Murphy 1996, 31).[3]

Niels Henrik Gregersen moves beyond Ellis and Murphy by explicitly arguing that supervenience is consistent with *top-down causality*.[4] In an unpublished article, 'Divine Action in a Universe of Minds,' he maintains a *holistic supervenience* that ascribes to consciousness a causal role capable of influencing behavior. Divine action occurs through the eucharistic experience such that there is both a transformation of mind, and a change in behavior (Gregersen 2000). It is obvious that Peacocke's embrace of top-down causality is compatible with Gregersen's understanding of supervenience. Novel, *holistic* properties emerging at higher levels can causally influence happenings at lower levels:

[3] Ellis and Murphy distinguish a *top-down effect* from a *top-down action*. The former occurs when 'conditions described at the higher semantic levels (such as macroscopic boundary conditions) determine the detailed evolution of a system' (Ellis and Murphy 1996, 25). The latter happens only when there is a contra-causally free agent exercising its control through top-down effects (op. cit., 36–7).

[4] The notion of top-down causality was originally introduced by D. Campbell in 1974 in discussing hierarchically organized biological systems. Peacocke makes wide appeal to the concept, even suggesting that 'God can exert continuous top-down causative influences on the world-as-a-whole in a way analogous to that whereby we in our thinking can exert effects on our bodies in a "top-down" manner' (1993, 161). There are criticisms of the concept within the theology–science discussion, e.g. see Drees (1996, 101–4) and Bielfeldt (1999 and 2000).

the changes at the microlevel, that of the constituent units, are what they are *because* of their incorporation into the system as a whole, which is exerting specific constraints on its units, making them behave otherwise than they would in isolation (Peacocke 1993, 53–4)

In two recent articles, I argue for the centrality of supervenience for the science–theology discussion, suggesting that God's relationship to the world can be understood as supervenient insofar as it constitutes a *metaphysical part–whole* relation, rather than a *causal temporal* one (Bielfeldt 1995, 5).[5] Beginning with the assumption that God and universe should not be understood as distinct ontic domains (but as two distinguishable *layers* within one domain), I claim God's actions can be understood as supervenient upon natural physical processes such that *intralevel causality* is allowed, but *interlevel causality* denied.[6] My view thus rejects *downward causation*, while claiming a *physical monism* of events and entities and a *conceptual pluralism* of properties and relations. I believe that supervenience is attractive for theology for at least three reasons: (1) it does not imply *reductionism*, the traditional foe of theology; (2) it rejects *dualism*, and its seemingly intractable problem of the causal interaction between God and the universe; and (3) it promises the granting of *truth conditions* to theological language by providing requisite constraints on the ascription of divine terms.[7]

---

[5] I emphasized there and in Bielfeldt (1999) that I was thereby modeling only divine *immanence*. I suggested that divine *transcendence* could perhaps be accounted for by appealing to a phenomenological ontology which would distinguish in a Tillichian way between the *structure* and *depth* of being. Of course, while Being-Itself transcends any ontic entity or event, it can have by definition no causal connection to any entity or event (Bielfeldt 1995, 11).

[6] Assume two levels, one having physical properties P and the other having divine properties D. The idea is that only entities having P are causally related physically, and only those individuals possessing divine properties (or having properties relatable to the divine) – level D – are causally related divinely. On this view, an evolutionary account of natural processes can be causally closed physically, while yet possessing a supervening level of divine entities and causally connected events referred to by the language of divine creation. The same reality can thus be referred to by multiple levels of description. Specifically excluded are causal relations between P and D entities and events.

[7] I have in mind the problem of meaningfulness of First Article statements, and the difficulty of locating those statements with respect to other kinds of discourse. On the basis of the supervenience relation, divine properties of creation covary with respect to the properties of natural evolution, such that for

It is important to note, however, that my use of 'supervenience' differs significantly from Gregersen's in that I explicitly reject what he embraces: the possibility of downward causation.[8] Given this difference, the question arises as to what *ought* the relationship be between supervenience and downward causation (or downward effects and action): does supervenience entail downward causation, its denial, or neither? More broadly, we must ask the following: What exactly *is* supervenience, and what fruit does it bear in the science–theology conversation?

Unfortunately, an answer to this question is not easy, for as Jaegwon Kim remarked in 1990, 'supervenience is almost exclusively a philosopher's concept, one not likely to be encountered outside philosophical dissertations and disputations' (Kim 1993, 131). However, because of the increasing use of supervenience within the science–theology dialogue, participants in that discussion must now get clear on exactly what this 'philosopher's concept' means. To that end, this essay looks at the notion of supervenience as it is currently employed within contemporary analytical philosophy, and speculates as to its appropriation for the science–theology discussion. My paper has three more sections: II briefly traces the development of the concept of supervenience; III examines some of the important philosophical issues confronting it; and IV briefly speculates about the peril and promise of supervenience for theology.

II. The Concept of Supervenience

The *Oxford English Dictionary* lists 1594 as the first documented use of the adjective *supervenient*, 1647–8 for the verb *supervene*, and 1664

---

the eyes of faith, statements about God's mighty acts in history are not merely arbitrary, but instead have definite conditions of assertability and truth.

[8] This has led him to call my view an example of *physicalist supervenience* (Gregersen 2000). I am not entirely unhappy with this label because, as will become evident, the very concept of supervenience entails bottom-up determination. I believe that true top-down causality violates the spirit of supervenience because it makes the specific actualization of the subvenient level dependent upon the state of the supervenient level. At least this is true given certain realist assumptions about the nature of the subvenient and supervenient groups.

for the noun *supervenience*. All of these uses apply to concrete occurrences and connote the extraneous or additional 'coming upon' of a given event, as in, 'Upon a sudden supervened the death of the king' (1647–8). Dr Samuel Johnson's *A Dictionary of the English Language* (1775) also points out that *supervene* means 'to come as an extraneous addition,' and *Webster's New International Dictionary* (1986) defines it as 'coming or occurring as something additional, extraneous, or unexpected.' Notice that in all these uses the supervenient event occurs after the event upon which it supervenes. In other words, all of these presuppose temporal order.[9]

This vernacular usage has little, however, to do with the way the term has come to be used within contemporary philosophy. Jaegwon Kim, the most important contributor to the supervenience literature, finds the first modern philosophical use of *supervene* (*supervenire*) in Leibniz's treatment of relations. Leibniz writes:

> Relation is an accident which is in multiple subjects; it is what results without any change made in the subjects but supervenes from them; it is the thinkability of objects together when we think of multiple things simultaneously.[10]

As Kim points out, while this statement could be interpreted as consistent with the reducibility of relations to the 'intrinsic denominations' of things, it might also be construed as asserting that relations supervene on the intrinsic qualities of their relata (Kim 1993, 136).

It is generally agreed that G. E. Moore was the first to employ the concept of supervenience (though not the actual term) in characterizing the relationship between moral and natural properties:

> if a given thing possesses any kind of intrinsic value in a certain degree, then not only must that thing possess it, under all circumstances, in the same degree, but also anything exactly like it, must, under all possess it in exactly the same degree. (Kim 1993, 261)

---

[9] I owe this word study to Kim. For more see Kim (1993, 131–2).
[10] See Kim (1993, 135–6). The Latin text reads: 'Relatio est accidens quod est in pluribus subjectie estque resultans tantum sue nulla mutatione facta ab iis supervenit, si plura simul cogitantur, est concogitabilitas.' See *Die Leibniz-Handschriften der königlichen öffentlichen Bibliothek zu Hannover*, ed. E. Bodemann, Hanover, 1895, VIII.c.74.

According to this formulation, there can be no difference in the distribution of moral properties without some difference in behaviors, temperament, etc. Clearly, Moore had anticipated the view that moral properties supervene upon natural ones.[11]

Hare is usually credited with having first explicitly used 'supervenience,' though he claims that it was already at use at Oxford at the time:[12]

> First, let us take that characteristic of 'good' which has been called its supervenience. Suppose that we say 'St. Francis was a good man'. It is logically impossible to say this and to maintain at the same time that there might have been another man placed exactly in the same circumstances as St. Francis, and who behaved in exactly the same way, but who differed from St. Francis in this respect only, that he was not a good man. (Hare 1952, 145)

Hare clearly claims that it is impossible for two people to possess the same natural properties in the same circumstances yet possess different ethical properties. We could not say that 'Oscar was *not* a good man' if Oscar behaved exactly like St Francis in exactly the same circumstances. For Moore and Hare, both the *covariance* between the moral and natural properties, and the *definitional nonreducibility* of the former to the latter are important (Kim 1993, 137).[13]

Supervenience was introduced into the philosophy of mind by Donald Davidson in his seminal 1970 article, 'Mental Events':

> mental characteristics are in some sense dependent, or supervenient, on physical characteristics. Such supervenience might be taken to mean that there cannot be two events alike in all physical respects but differing in some mental respect, or that an object cannot alter in some

---

[11] Kim also quotes Sidgwick as foreshadowing the contemporary use of supervenience as talking about properties or characteristics which covary with respect to each other: 'We cannot judge an action to be right for A and wrong for B, unless we can find in the nature or circumstances of the two some difference which we can regard as a reasonable ground for difference in their duties' (Kim 1993, 136).

[12] In his 1984 Inaugural Address to the Aristotelian Society, Hare (1984) says that although he was not the first to use *supervenience* in its current philosophical sense, he could not point to any particular philosopher who had employed the term.

[13] See Armstrong (1989, 103) for another statement of supervenience's commitment to covariance.

mental respect without altering in some physical respect. Dependence or supervenience of this kind does not entail reducibility through law or definition: if it did, we could reduce moral properties to descriptive, and this there is good reason to *believe* cannot be done; and we might be able to reduce truth in a formal system to syntactical properties, and this we *know* cannot in general be done. (Davidson 1980, 214)

Davidson explicitly says that supervenience is a dependency relation that does not entail *nomological reducibility* (i.e. there are no laws that correlate mental states and brain states). By granting a degree of autonomy to the mental in a physicalist universe, Davidson thus advances his *anomalous monism*. While physical particulars exhaust the inventory of what ultimately exists, there are mental properties which, though they cannot be biconditionally linked to any particular physical actualizations, are nonetheless realizable within some set of physical processes.

As Kim repeatedly points out, the three ideas of *covariance*, *dependency*, and *nonreducibility* are closely associated with supervenience. With Moore and Hare we get covariance and definitional nonreducibility, while with Davidson we add dependency and nomological nonreducibility. Kim summarizes the three components of supervenience as follows (Kim 1993, 140):

> *Covariance*: Supervenient properties covary with their subvenient, or base, properties. In particular, indiscernibility in respect of the base properties entails indiscernibility in respect of the supervenient properties.
>
> *Dependency*: Supervenient properties are dependent on, or are determined by, their base properties.
>
> *Nonreducibility*: Supervenience is to be consistent with the irreducibility of supervenient properties to their base properties.[14]

But are these three notions compatible? In the third section of the paper we will examine the relationships between covariance and dependency, and between dependency and reduction.

---

[14] Strictly speaking, it seems that *dependency* and *determinacy* are two different relations. Consider A_1 and A_2 as events in system S having certain laws such that A_2 happens only if A_1 occurs. Now clearly A_2 is dependent upon A_1. But does A_1 determine A_2? It need not, for suppose A_1 can occur without A_2 happening. In other words, A_2 is dependent upon A_1 if and only if A_1 is *necessary* for A_2, but A_2 is determined by A_1 if and only if A_1 is *sufficient* for A_2 (Grimes 1995, 83).

The post-Davidson discussion of supervenience has been quite lively, with Hellman and Thompson (1975), Armstrong (1982), Horgan (1982), Haugeland (1982), Teller (1984a), Currie (1984), Petrie (1987), and Grimes (1988) all providing early and important contributions. Kim, however, has been the most influential voice within the supervenience discussion over the last twenty years, because his careful work has basically established the contour of the supervenience landscape.[15] All of these writers have emphasized the importance of the notion of determination or dependency for supervenience: for S to be supervenient upon P, it must somehow be determined by P. Paul Teller clearly articulates this dependency in the passage below:

> Imagine that in some given case or situation you get to play God and decide what's true. To organize your work you divide truths into two (not necessarily exhaustive) kinds. The first you call truths of kind P ... and the second you call truths of kind S ... You begin your work by choosing all the truths of kind P which will hold for the case. Then you turn to the truths of kind S. But lo! Having chosen truths of kind P, the truths of kind S have already been fixed ... This allegory presents the core idea of what people have described under the names of 'supervenience' and 'determination'. (Teller 1984a, 137)

It should be obvious from this quote that supervenience without determination is not supervenience at all. In other words, the concept of supervenience entails determination.

It must be pointed out, however, that the British emergentist tradition of the 1920s used 'supervenience' in a somewhat different manner from that of the post-Davidson discussion. According to Kim, the term was used by C. Lloyd Morgan and others as an 'occasional stylistic variant' in speaking about 'the emergent.'[16] Stephen C. Pepper in a 1926 article entitled 'Emergence' in the *Journal of Philosophy* writes:

---

[15] See Kim (1993) for a collection of his most important articles.

[16] Kim 1993, 134. Kim does not seem to think their usages are distinct: 'the concept he [Lloyd Morgan] intended with these terms seems surprisingly close to the supervenience concept current today.' I believe, however, that McLaughlin is correct in pointing out that the two uses of supervenience are really quite different (McLaughlin 1995, 50; 1992).

there is emergence, which is a cumulative change, a change in which certain characteristics supervene upon other characteristics, these characteristics being adequate to explain the occurrence on their level. (Pepper 1926, 241)

Here 'supervenience' just means 'emergent'. The supervening properties are those which emerge from the subvenient properties, and which can be explained by those properties.[17] If A emerges from B, then A supervenes upon B. Lloyd Morgan explicitly uses 'supervenience' in characterizing Samuel Alexander's view of the emergence of spatiotemporal events and deity (Morgan 1926, 9 and 30). Accordingly, spatiotemporal events supervene on physical and chemical events, and deity supervenes on reflective consciousness. While emergents are not reducible to their basal conditions, when the appropriate basal conditions are present the emergents come into existence.

While both the British Emergentists and the post-Davidson discussion understand that subvening properties determine supervenient ones without thereby reducing the latter to the former, there is an important difference between their corresponding supervenience notions. The emergentists are committed to *downward causation* in a way in which contemporary supervenience is not. The British Emergentists clearly assume the nomological possibility of higher-level kinds influencing the motion of lower-level kinds in ways that cannot be predicted by the laws governing those latter kinds (McLaughlin 1992, 51). But if this is so, then the distribution of B properties are determined by the distribution of A properties, such that one cannot simply say 'A supervenes upon B.' I would claim that supervenience implies an *asymmetrical* dependency relation that is broken by downward causation.[18]

---

[17] Pepper actually sets forward a critique of the autonomy of supervenient emergentism which is not unlike that lodged against it today. He argues persuasively that if supervenient characteristics survive, they must survive as mere epiphenomena, for if these characteristics are cumulative 'over and above the degrees of integration,' or if the 'marks of [the] higher [cannot be deduced] from those of the lower level,' then they are epiphenomenal (241).

[18] Because Kim believes that contemporary nonreductive physicalism is also committed to downward causation, he does not find different understandings of supervenience in the emergentists and the post-Davidson discussion (Kim

While the 'upward determination' of A by B seems to imply super-venience, the 'downward causation' from A to B suggests other-wise.[19] Supervenience, in my opinion, cannot be a 'two-way street'.[20]

Interestingly, this latter use of 'supervenience' appears to have quite a history. Alexander of Aphrodisias, teaching in Athens in AD 200, rejected the identity of the soul with the simple combination of primary bodies, declaring instead that it 'is a vital force that comes into being as an addition to the combination' (Grimes 1995, 120–1).[21] It is this concept of 'vital force' that arises in all discussion to top-down causation. The question is this: Is there in the emergent, some power or disposition that can affect lower level actualizations, a power or force neither epistemologically nor ontologically reducible to lower-level events and processes? In the next section we will take up this issue as we rehearse standard formulations of the supervenience relation.

1992). Unfortunately, the claim that nonreductive physicalism is committed to downward causation is controversial and its adjudication beyond the scope of this essay. It should be pointed out, however, that the British Emergentists emphasize downward causation much more explicitly than do contemporary nonreductive physicalists. If McLaughlin is correct, they could specify a 'scientific basis' for it that is not possible for current nonreductive physicalism (McLaughlin 1992, 89–91).

[19] Kim claims that 'emergentism therefore entails a supervenience doctrine: all aspects of a given thing, or even of the whole world, are fixed once its total physical character is fixed' (Kim 1992, 124). Yet how can this be true if 'in spite of this ontological dependence, [the higher level] begins to lead a causal life of its own, with a capacity to influence that which sustains its very existence?' (Kim 1992, 137).

[20] While Miller (1990) argues that the supervenient can also determine the subvenient, Hellman (1992) argues persuasively that it cannot. It should be noted that 'downward causation' does not arise directly in this philo-sophical discussion at all. Rather, the question is whether dependency asymmetricality is violated when we allow the supervenient language the same richness and capacity for fine-tuning as we do the subvenient language.

[21] See Athanasios P. Fotinis, *The* De Anima *of Alexander of Aphrodisias: A Trans-lation and Commentary*, Washington DC, 36, quoted in Grimes 1995, 121. Grimes also points out that Donatus used *supervenio* in his 1445 Latin translation of Alexander's *De Anima* to translate passages where Alexander speaks about the relation between the soul and primary bodies.

III.　Philosophical Issues Confronting Supervenience

Given that 'supervenience' can sustain different interpretations, what is the common meaning it possesses in the contemporary discussion? The core idea is expressed clearly by McLaughlin:

> Thus, A-respects supervene on B-respects if and only if exact similarity in B-respects excludes the possibility of difference in A-respects. So, for example, mental respects supervene on physical respects if and only if exact similarity in every physical respect excludes the possibility of difference in any mental respect. (McLaughlin 1995, 17)

This description clearly displays determination. Because the A-respects of two objects cannot differ if their B-respects are the same, the A-respects are presumably determined by their B-respects. Note the asymmetricality: while the B-respects of two objects can differ and their A-respects remain the same, the converse does not hold.

In the above formulation McLaughlin uses 'respect' so as not to prejudice the metaphysical issue about what the relata of the supervenience relationship ultimately are. Although Kim believes properties constitute those relata, this is only because he understands properties quite broadly as that which any meaningful predicate expresses. But if property is construed as an ontological category, it is not at all clear that properties can be relata. For his part, Davidson has opted for predicates as the relata. Other suggestions include truths (Teller 1984a), states of affairs, events (Davidson 1980, 214), facts (Chalmers 1996, 33), world-regions (Horgan 1982), languages (Haugeland 1982; Bonevac 1988 and 1995), propositions (Bacon 1986, 170), and entities in general (Armstrong 1989, 103). In what follows, I will assume that properties are the relata of the supervenience relation, and will use the term in a *pleonastic* sense to designate that which is expressed by a predicate.

In the burgeoning literature on supervenience a number of important distinctions have been made, of which the following are especially significant for the science–theology discussion: (1) *strong, weak,* and *global* supervenience; (2) *modal* v. *possible worlds* construals of each; (3) *ontological* v. *ascriptive* supervenience; (4) *supervenience* and *covariance*; (5) the relation between *supervenience* and *reduction*. I will discuss each in turn.

Strong, Weak, and Global Supervenience

Weak supervenience is perhaps easiest to explain, so I will begin there. It is basically the claim that within any particular world, two things indiscernible with respect to their lower-level properties, are indiscernible with respect to their higher-level properties. Alternately, if there is some difference in higher-level properties, there must be some difference in lower-level properties. The following formulation by Kim captures this:

> (WS$_m$) A *weakly supervenes* on B if and only if, necessarily, for any object x and any property F in A, if x has F, then there exists a property G in B such that x has G, and if any y has G, it has F. (Kim 1993, 80)

This formulation captures a 'necessity of consequence' between B and A, that is, necessarily if some object has both A and B, for all objects having B, then they have A (Blackburn 1984, 184). What weak supervenience rules out are possible worlds in which objects have both B and A, and B and not-A. Weak supervenience prohibits placing in the same world B-duplicates which are not A-duplicates. It still allows, however, the creating of B-duplicates that are not A-duplicates, if they are in different worlds. Weak supervenience thus offers *intra-world* but not *cross-world* constraint (Kim 1994, 577).

Strong supervenience asserts cross-world or inter-world constraint by claiming a *rigid covariance* of lower-level and upper-level properties. Again I offer Kim's characterization:

> (SS$_m$) A *strongly supervenes* on B if and only if, necessarily, for any object x and any property F in A, if x has F, then there exists a property G in B such that x has G, and *necessarily* if any y has G, it has F. (Kim 1993, 80)

This expresses a 'necessitation of the consequent,' that is, necessarily, for all y, if y has B then y has A (Blackburn 1984, 184). The advantage to strong supervenience is that it supports counterfactuals. It says, for instance, that if the lower-level state were to be B, then the higher-level state would be A. Without this inter-worldly constraint, the higher-level properties could vary widely with respect to a minor lower-level change, or not vary at all. Because of its ability to sustain counterfactuals, a number of writers claim that genuine determination can only be captured by strong supervenience.

In order to see why this is so, consider Fred and his molecule-by-molecule replica Fred*. According to WS_m, Fred and Fred* have a mental life that is indiscernible in this world, and in any other possible world in which they are both members. However, we might want to ask what would be the mental life of Fred* were he physically indiscernible to Fred when, in fact, he is not. According to WS_m, Fred and Fred* could have widely divergent mental lives, for there are no constraints placed on the assignment of mental properties when the individuals are located in two different possible worlds. But this result seems incompatible with the thesis of neurophysiological determination of the mental.

The same problem arises on the ascription of ethical properties. Assume that Ann and Ann* are physical replicas. (All their behaviors and dispositions are the same.) Then on WS_m, Ann and Ann* have the same ethical properties. However, what if Ann and Ann* are *not* replicas, and the question is nevertheless asked 'Would Ann* have been good *were* she to have done what Ann did?' On WS_m Ann* need not be good. But this seems to contradict basic moral intuitions. Therefore, it seems WS_m is too weak to capture the strong determination presupposed in each of these cases.

Now consider a famous painting and a molecule-by-molecule replica of it that is a forgery. On both WS_m and SS_m, the economic value of each painting should be the same. Yet clearly the original is worth far more than the forgery. The apparent failure of supervenience is due to the problem of circumscribing the subvenient base. Since the economic value of the painting involves a relationship to its environment (e.g. by whom and when it was painted, etc.), the subvenient base must be extended so as to include its relation to that environment. To expect the price of the painting to supervene only upon the intrinsic properties of the object is to demand that a *relational* property can supervene on *nonrelational* ones. But there is no reason to expect that nonintrinsic, relational properties supervene on intrinsic, nonrelational ones.[22] If one

---

[22] Putnam's twin earth example surely shows this. Imagine that water on earth behaves just like 'twater' on twin earth, but that water on earth is H_2O, and on twin earth it is XYZ. Exact physical replicas identifying the substance on the two planets would nonetheless have different 'meanings' according to Putnam,

despairs of ever being able to specify the relational subvenient properties upon which the higher-level properties supervene, there is a third supervenience: *Global supervenience.*

While both weak and strong supervenience apply indiscernibility conditions *locally* (i.e. with respect to particular objects), this formulation expresses a *global* indiscernibility. Again we use Kim's formulation:

> (GS) A *globally supervenes* on B if and only if, any two worlds indiscernible with respect to B-properties are indiscernible with respect to A-properties. (Kim 1993, 82)

This type of supervenience is obviously more holistic than the other two. It is advocated most often by philosophers worried that weak supervenience is too weak to provide a robust sense of determination, while strong supervenience is too strong to avoid reductionism.

There is another issue that deserves attention here. WS_m and SS_m each apply indiscernibility locally, that is, each assume that sense can be made out of the very same thing having both A and B properties. But is not clear that the supervenience of the whole upon the parts (*mereological supervenience*) can make use of these formulations. If the whole supervenes upon its parts, then the individual(s) instantiating properties of the whole must differ from the individuals instantiating the properties of the parts. It seems that what is needed is a way to frame a supervenience relation across *multiple domains*, one domain consisting of wholes and the other consisting of their parts.

Kim has suggested the following multiple-domain supervenience relation where the supervenient properties distributed over the members of its domain get determined by the distribution of subvenient properties over members of its domain:

> (MS) $<A, D_1>$ supervenes on $<B, D_2>$ if and only if every complete distribution of B over D_2 entails a unique complete distribution of A over D_1. (Kim 1993, 113)

---

for the earthling would mean H_2O while his twin would mean XYZ (Putnam 1975). This shows that the relational property of meaning and belief cannot merely supervene on nonrelational neurophysiological states.

In the above formulation, allow A and B to be nonempty sets of properties, D_1 and D_2 to be nonempty sets of individuals, and the ordered pair to denote the distribution of the first member upon the second. Kim points out, however, that mereological is equivalent to global supervenience, if the latter is comprised of a fixed domain of individuals formed through the union of D_1 and D_2 (Kim 1993, 118). Accordingly, it is a type of holistic supervenience.[23]

Modal v. Possible Worlds Interpretations

Kim has argued that WS_m and SS_m are equivalent respectively to the following possible world formulations (Kim 1993, 81):

> (WS_p) A *weakly supervenes* on B if and only if, for any x and y, and for any possible world w, if x and y are B-indiscernible in w, they are A-indiscernible in w. (Kim 1993, 110)

> (SS_p) A *strongly supervenes* on B if and only if, for any x and y, and any worlds w and w*, if x in w is B-indiscernible from y in w*, then x in w is A-indiscernible form y in w*. (Kim 1993, 111)

As Brian McLaughlin points out, however, neither is WS_m equivalent to WS_p, nor is SS_m equivalent to SS_p. One problem is that quantifying over possible worlds does not allow a distinction between *logical, analytical, nomological,* and *metaphysically* possible worlds, even though logical, analytical, nomological, and metaphysical truths must be distinguished because of the fact that the explanations of why each are true differ (McLaughlin 1995, 26–7).

Regardless of this problem, it can be shown that if 'necessarily' in both SS_m and WS_m is taken as universal quantification over worlds, then the modal and possible world formulations of strong and weak supervenience are not equivalent, for while SS_m implies SS_p and WS_m implies WS_p, their converses do not hold (McLaughlin 1995, 27–30). For instance, WS_p would be trivially true if, in any possible world, no two entities had the same physical properties. (It would be true because the antecedent 'x and y are indiscernible

---

[23] The issue is further complicated by Kim's distinction between uncoordinated and coordinated multiple domains (Kim 1993, 123 ff.).

with respect to properties in B′ would be false, and any conditional with a false antecedent is true.) Yet WS_m could still be false, for there could be a world without physical properties that yet had a Cartesian ego. If this were so, then the phrase 'for any object x and for any property F in A, then there exists a property G in B,' would be false. Thus WS_p is true and WS_m is false. In like manner, the nonequivalence of the strong supervenience formulations can be shown. It should be emphasized, however, that this problem disappears if complementation is regarded as a legitimate property-forming operation.[24]

Ontological v. Ascriptive Supervenience

James Klagge has pointed out that supervenience relations are actually of two quite different types: *ontological* and *ascriptive*.

> Ontological supervenience is a connection between classes of properties (e.g. moral and natural properties), whereas ascriptive supervenience is a connection between types of judgments. Furthermore, in ontological supervenience the necessity of the connection involved is interpreted as being in the nature of things, or a metaphysical necessity. In ascriptive supervenience, on the other hand, the necessity is interpreted as a conceptual or logical requirement. (Klagge 1988, 462)

Ontological supervenience (OS) differs from ascriptive supervenience (AS) in that the first says that things cannot differ with respect to their supervenient properties without also differing with respect to their subvenient properties, while the latter claims that one's *judgements* about a supervening thing cannot differ unless one's judgements about the subvenient thing were to differ. According to Klagge, 'two things, even in the same possible world, could be judged descriptively indiscernible and yet receive different moral valuations if they were judged by different people employing different moral principles' (Klagge 1988, 463). AS differs from OS in that the former constrains the judgements of a given person, while the latter constrains the judgement of all properly functioning

---

[24] See Van Cleve (1990) for an argument against the equivalence of the modal and possible world formulations based upon an objection to Kim's use of the property-forming operation of complementation.

cognitive units. While OS assumes metaphysical necessity, AS speaks of conceptual or logical necessity. Obviously, AS is open to an antirealist construal, for 'from the fact that it is reasonable to place certain constraints on our judgements, it does not follow that the world is constituted in any particular way' (Klagge 1988, 464). Another difference is that AS but not OS explicitly asserts an evidential relationship between its classes of properties. For instance, the mental ontologically supervenes on the brain, but the latter does not normally count as criteria for the ascribing of the mental – though behavior does do so. In the case of the moral, however, natural behaviors and dispositions serve as the very criteria by which to ascribe certain ethical qualities to the person (Klagge 1988, 467).

Suppose one were an antirealist about moral properties. It would nevertheless hold that moral properties ascriptively strongly supervene upon natural properties for person S, if S consistently judges that x is good, when x has natural properties P and Q. Correspondingly, S could be an antirealist about the divine who nonetheless employs ascriptive strong supervenience to talk about specific divine action occurring 'in, with, and under' particular macrophysical actualizations. While S does not think that divine action is an intrinsic feature of the world, S nevertheless sees the world as if such agency were present.[25]

Supervenience and Covariance

While supervenience is supposed to involve an asymmetrical relation of dependency or determination, many philosophers believe that the standard formulations do not actually accomplish the task for which they were designed; instead they only provide

---

[25] I have in mind a construal of theological statements as *noncognitive*, that is, as expressions of the believer's attitudes which can nonetheless be consistently connected to each other and to factual statements in other types of discourse. Such a *quasi-realist* construal of theological language would parallel the ethical neo-expressionism of Blackburn (1984). For instance, one might claim the statement 'Jesus of Nazareth is the Son of God' is projected upon the world, for it is merely the expression of a salvific attitude towards that which confronts me with my being and the meaning of my being.

for the covariance of property groups.[26] Take, for instance, the supposed supervenience of the mental upon the physical. To say that if x and y are alike in physical respects they must be alike in mental respects is not either to explain why this relationship obtains or why the physical is more basic ontically than the mental.[27] It seems that anyone wanting to claim an ontic priority to the physical must appeal to something more than covariance; he or she must show how and why that covariance entails dependency.[28]

But there is perhaps even a stronger reason to assume that supervenience and covariance are logically independent. The definition of strong supervenience is satisfiable on the assumption

---

[26] It should be noted that the term 'covariance' does not really capture the notion that A-respects cannot vary without variation in B-respects, but that B-respects can vary without variation in A-respects. Perhaps the term *dependent-variation* is better. McLaughlin writes: 'The simple and easy idea of supervenience ... is ... *dependent-variation*, where the dependency is of a purely *modal* sort. Variation in A-respects depends on variation in B-respects in that A-respects *cannot* vary without variation in B-respects. Variation in the *supervenient* A-respects *requires* variation in the *subvenient* B-respects. A-respects *fail* to supervene on B-respects when and only when A-respects can vary *independently* of variations in B-respects' (1995, 18). While McLaughlin supposes that downward causation violates the spirit of supervenience, it is not clear that it violates this particular criterion. The fact that A *causes* B to be other than it would have been does not entail that A can vary independently of B, for A could not do this if B had not already determined A. The issue is complex and obviously needs more study. Perhaps McLaughlin's criterion should be weakened from 'when and only when A-respects' to 'when A-respects'.

[27] Grimes (1988) argues that none of the supervenience formulations adequately captures the intuition that differences in B-respects explain differences in A-respects.

[28] For example, Terrence Horgan (1993) attempts to provide an account of supervenience that incorporates materialist explanations of the supervening properties. McLaughlin suggests one might strengthen the core idea of supervenience such 'that we have supervenience of A-respects on B-respects when and only when there could be no difference of sort A without some further difference of sort B that *makes it the* case that there is the difference of sort A in question' (McLaughlin 1995, 18). Others suggest, however, that supervenience must not always include an explanatory relation. Even Kim occasionally admits that supervenience might sometimes constitute a 'brute fact', a primitive, unexplainable relation of dependency between property groups (Kim 1993, 156). Cf. the British Emergentists' notion that the relationship between the emergent property and its base must be accepted, in Alexander's famous words, 'with natural piety' (Kim 1992, 126).

of psychophysical parallelism, a form of dualism rejecting any causal or metaphysical interaction between realms (Savellos and Yalcin 1995, 10). But if the strong supervenience formulation is satisfiable both on the assumption of psychophysical parallelism and materialism, then there seems to be nothing within standard supervenience formulations that capture the desired metaphysical determination or dependency of the supervening A properties on the subvenient B properties.

The reason why this is so is that oftentimes when speaking of determination and dependency we are speaking about mere *functional dependence*. For instance, in $f(x) = x^3 + 1$, the value of $f(x)$ depends on, or is determined by the value of x in $x^3 + 1$, without there being any asymmetrical metaphysical dependency. Even if one were to advance Kim's proposal in hopes of capturing the desired asymmetry, there are still many problems:

> (SD) A-properties depend on B-properties just in case A strongly covaries with B, but not conversely; that is, any B-indiscernible things are A-indiscernible but there are A-indiscernible things that are B-discernible. (Kim 1993, 145)

As Kim himself points out, imagine a case where there is correlation between A-properties and B-properties that run only one way. For example, it seems that intelligence (A) covaries with manual dexterity (B), but not conversely. We would not want to say, however, that intelligence is determined by manual dexterity, because the real explanation involves some further C-properties: genetic and developmental factors (Kim 1993, 146). To the response that SD can be strengthened by adding 'provided there is not a set C upon which A and B severally depend,' the ready rejoinder is that 'depend' has now been used in the analysis. Circularity seems to scuttle any effort to find an analysis for supervenience capturing asymmetric dependency.[29]

The upshot of all of this is that one could claim that all of the popular supervenience definitions are really definitions of covariance, and not definitions of supervenience at all. Notice, however,

---

[29] Bonevac (1995, 131 ff.) takes issue with Kim's arguments for strong supervenience not capturing dependence.

that even if the definitions of supervenience are inadequate because they do not protect against all counter-examples, it does not really change what is included in the concept of supervenience. Supervenience is *supposed* to be a dependency relation, regardless of how well the popular formulations capture that relation.

Supervenience and Reduction

The question as to whether or not supervenience determination implies reduction is a hot one. While supervenience was originally employed by proponents wanting to escape the philosophical horrors of reduction, it appears that on certain interpretations of 'reduction,' some of the supervenience formulations are reductionistic. In order to see this, we must distinguish senses of reduction (Horgan 1995, 438).

Ontological reduction asserts that there are identities between the entities, events, kinds, properties and facts referred to respectively by the higher-level and the lower-level discourse. For instance, if there are only classes, then all higher-level entities posited in classical mathematics are ontologically reducible to them. Similarly, if there are only neurophysiological events, then all mental processes and states are ontologically reducible to those events.

Conceptual or *semantic reduction* holds that there are semantic equivalences between statements of the higher-level and lower-level discourse. *Phenomenalism* claimed that every statement about the physical world is semantically equivalent to some set of statements about actual or possible experience. Similarly, *logical* or *analytical behaviorism* maintained that each and every mental conduct term could be given a semantically equivalent definition in terms of some set of statements about actual or possible behavior. Thus, when Davidson claims that his anomalous monism couples claims of ontological monism and conceptual dualism, he is maintaining that mental *ontologically* but not *semantically* reduces to the neurophysiological (Davidson 1980, 231).

Scientific or *nomological reduction* declares that laws or states of affairs posited by a higher-level theory are explainable by those described in some other scientific theory. For instance, thermodynamic theory is scientifically reducible to the theory of mechanics because heat is explainable in terms of the movement and vibration of particles. Because transfer of heat can be explained by the laws governing the motion transfer of atoms, thermodynamic explanations are subsumable under mechanical explanations. Such a *nomological reduction* is really a type of ontological reduction, although it has an empirical nature. It is only because we have epistemic access to both the phenomena of mechanics and thermodynamics that we can make the appropriate identification. One might argue, however, that there are ontic regions for which we will never have the requisite epistemic access, and yet there is still ontological reduction. For instance, although we perhaps never will have access both to the mental and neurophysiological so as to allow nomic reduction of the former to the latter, the former is nonetheless ontologically reducible to the latter. Davidson claims that despite the absence of psychophysical bridge laws, the physical comprises all that ultimately exists. His anomalous monism thus asserts both a conceptual and scientific nonreducibility.[30]

Kim has argued that strong supervenience entails necessary coextension and thus nomological reducibility. Suppose that A-properties supervene on B-properties. Thus, when x has B_1, it also has a property A_i, such that B_1 is *sufficient* for A_i. But since A_i is *multiply realizable*, B_2 or B_3 or .... B_n are also sufficient for A_i. According to Kim, the union of all B_i is thus *necessarily sufficient* for A_i, i.e. A_i if and only if B_1 v B_2 v B_3 ... B_n. If we allow the formation of infinite disjunctions of subvenient properties, then there is *necessary coextension*, the mark of nomological reduction (Kim 1993, 149–55).

Teller, Post and others have argued that infinitary disjunction is not a property-forming operation, and hence this putative reduction does not follow (Teller 1984a; Post 1984). If one assumes that the complexity and artificiality of the union of all B properties counts against its genuineness, one might reject UB_i as a reduction base. But I am not sure this move works, for from the fact that

---

[30] Other reduction typologies might be employed. Searle distinguishes *ontological, property, theoretical, logical* and *causal reduction* (Searle 1992, 113–15). Peacocke identifies *methodological, epistemological* and *ontological reduction* (Peacocke 1976).

humans have an epistemic limitation regarding the specification of the infinite disjunction of B properties each sufficient for A_i, it does not follow that there exists no infinite disjunction and concomitant ontological reduction.[31]

Even if Kim is wrong, however, and necessary coextension is disallowed between A-properties and B-properties, it is still not clear that reduction can be avoided. It was Ernest Nagel's *Structure of Science* that set prevailing opinions about what constitutes reduction. According to Nagel, theory T_1 reduces T_2 if and only if all the laws of T_2 can be derived from the laws of T_1 by virtue of bridge laws connecting terms of the two theories. However, as Thomas Grimes has pointed out, nowhere does Nagel suggest that these bridge laws must be biconditional. Instead, 'a simple derivation of the former from the latter by means of lawlike one-way conditionals will do' (Grimes 1995, 112). If this is so, then it seems as if strong supervenience and global supervenience might be reductive relations after all.

All the issues of this section are obviously quite philosophical, and many remain controversial in the literature. I suggest, however, that the use of 'supervenience' by participants in the science–theology discussion must be informed by these issues. For instance, it is not clear that weak supervenience is a dependency relation; it is uncertain whether strong and global supervenience can avoid reducibility; it is not obvious that covariance can provide an adequate basis for dependency; and it is extremely dubious whether or not downward causation is compatible with the spirit of supervenience. What positions are adopted on these issues will determine in part one's evaluation of the fruitfulness of super-venience for relating science and theology.

---

[31] Bonevac (1995) uses the image of divine knowledge to flesh out the distinction the realist asserts between real ontological reduction and scientific reduction: 'If we think of supervenience as reduction in the mind of God as ... a realist might, then we can identify mental and physical states without believing that we will ever possess, or could even possess, strict psychophysical laws linking the mental and physical realms ... From God's perspective, the mental and physical would be linked by strict biconditional laws, but those laws might be so complex that they are humanly incomprehensible' (138).

IV. Perils and Promises for Theology

So what value might supervenience have for the science–theology discussion? I believe that it is potentially fruitful in the following ways: (1) supervenience's rejection of dualism and embrace of a layered approach to reality suggests a way to understand divine agency and action as *not* interfering with the natural order, and thus *not* violating causal closure requirements; (2) the use of supervenience to relate science and theology is consistent with an *explanatory compatibilism* widely acknowledged among the natural sciences themselves; (3) supervenience suggests the *nonreducibility* of the whole to the part, and thus seems to allow the ascription of ontological status to the realm of value and purpose, a realm extremely important to religion.

But supervenience is also problematic for the science–theology discussion in at least three ways: (1) the supervenience of the divine upon the physical implies that the universe determines God, and not that God determines the universe; (2) employing the problematic notion of downward causation with supervenience violates the spirit (if not the letter) of supervenience; (3) the supervenience of the whole on the part may actually be consistent with microreduction and materialism. We will look at each in turn. Let us begin with the positive.

The supervenience of the divine upon natural processes could be conceived as analogous to the supposed supervenience of the mental on the neurophysiological. As used in the philosophy of mind, supervenience is thought to be compatible with the following claims: *physical monism* (all concrete particulars are physical); *antireductionism* (mental properties are not reducible to physical properties); *physical realization* (all mental properties are physically realized, e.g. whenever mental property M is instantiated, there is some physical property P which realizes M); and *mental realism* (mental properties are not merely instrumental, but are real properties of events and objects) (Kim 1993, 344).[32] Analogously,

---

[32] The question, of course, is whether or not these claims really are compatible. See Kim's argument that they are not (Kim 1993, 336–57).

the theologian might embrace *physical monism*, the *irreducibility* of the divine to the physical, the *realization* of divine agency and action within the physical, and the *reality* of divine agency and action. Just as contemporary philosophy of mind claims that human agency and action is real, irreducible, yet realizable within a monistic physical domain, so might the theologian argue that divine agency and action has the same characteristics. Just as the 'I' is real, transcendent and irreducible, yet physically realized within the brain, so might God be real, transcendent and irreducible, yet physically realizable within the universe (Bielfeldt 1995 and 1999). Such a strategy develops Peacocke's suggestion of God's 'transcendence-in-immanence' (Peacocke 1979, 131–7; 1984, 73–8).

In working with this analogy one might try out different supervenience formulations. Does God weakly, strongly, or globally supervene upon the universe? In what sense does He supervene? Is the supervenient relation *conceptual* or *metaphysical*? Must we talk about different domains with God as the *whole* and the universe as the *parts*? Are we speaking about a real ontological supervenience of the divine, or merely an ascriptive supervenience about how we are constrained to talk about the divine?

While this supervenience strategy may seem shocking to some, I would argue that it actually provides a more robust notion of deity than that encountered in much of the post-Kantian tradition, where the divine is wholly stripped of causal power.[33] In any case this use of divine supervenience seems not completely unlike that of Samuel Alexander in *Space, Time, and Deity*, where deity is figured as 'the next higher empirical quality to mind, which the universe is engaged in bringing to birth' (Alexander 1979, II.347), or where 'God's body is at any stage the whole Space-Time, of which the finites that enter into God's body are but specialized complexes' (366).

---

[33] Kant's argument that neither the category of cause or substantiality applies to God was assumed by subsequent German theology. This assumption resulted in a number of theological options which tried to conceive divine agency and action noncausally.

Second, the use of supervenience seems to be consistent with the explanatory compatibilism of the natural sciences. The notion is that a set of events can be given a physical, chemical, biochemical, biological, psychological, sociological, political, or economic explanation. If this is true, why not permit theology again to be queen of the sciences by allowing a highest-level theological explanation of that same set of events? Through the use of supervenience, theological language could perhaps reclaim its traditional task of explaining why things are what they are, and thus escape the charge of being merely a 'ghetto language' disconnected from everything else. An explanatory language has relevance in people's lives. To the degree that theology continues to spurn talk of cause and explanation, it becomes increasingly marginalized in the lives of many; it becomes a 'wheel idly turning.'

Third, supervenience's commitment to nonreducibility is attractive to theologians and scientists searching for a way to ascribe ontological status to value, meaning and purpose in a universe that seems at bottom to be physical. The intuition that the whole is somehow greater than the sum of its parts is very powerful, and it can result in strong claims of holism, claims which assert that the higher-level reality is not merely conceptually or nomologically irreducible to the lower level, but that it is somehow ontologically irreducible as well.[34] If higher-level reality is invested with causal power such that it can affect actualizations at the lower level, then it is not *ontologically reducible* to the latter, for the causal powers that arise at that higher level are *sui generis*.[35] As the British Emergentists would say, they are not mere *resultants*, but rather are *emergents*.[36] If the emergentist tradition's understanding of

---

[34] One needs to specify the sense of *ontological irreducibility*. One might argue for an ontological property irreducibility or causal irreducibility, while yet admitting an ontological constitutive reducibility.

[35] Again, one might allow constitutive reducibility while denying property and causal reducibility.

[36] The Emergentists claimed that an effect is *emergent* 'if and only if it is not the sum of the types of effects ... each type of cause has' (McLaughlin 1992, 65). This contrasts with a *resultant* where the effect is calculable given the types of causes comprising it. This distinction has led to confusion, because it seems to suggest that the Emergentists claim an effect is emergent *because* it is unpredictable. But I follow McLaughlin in emphasizing the *ontological* character of

supervenience is assumed (i.e. there are genuine emergents with powers of downward causation), then the supervenience concept may indeed breathe new life into the science–theology discussion. If mental events can 'downwardly cause' behavior, and if culture itself can 'downwardly cause' particular mental events, why not posit a God who can 'downwardly influence' the values, meanings, and purposes of culture?

It is important to notice the different way in which 'supervenience' is used in these strategies. While options I and II seem best to fit the notion of supervenience as it is employed in the post-Davidson discussion, option III clearly assumes the British Emergentist construal of supervenience. I believe that further work in disentangling these two senses of supervenience will pay handsome dividends in evaluating the potential fruitfulness of supervenience for the science–theology conversation.

As was previously mentioned, however, there are some caveats as well. The first point is really quite obvious. If theological reality supervenes on physical reality, then physical entities and properties end up *determining* divine reality. But this seems to get things exactly backwards, for the theist's central claim is that there is a God distinct from the universe who nonetheless creates the universe, sustains it in being, and ultimately redeems it through His own incarnation. Perhaps it is time to admit that the major Western monotheisms are inescapably committed to *ontological dualism* – no matter how philosophically unfashionable and scientifically suspect that prospect is (Bielfeldt 2000).

The second caveat pertains to the use of *downward causation* by supervenience advocates. Besides the problem of the semantic compatibility of the two notions, the larger problem arises concerning downward causality's meaning and coherence. The

---

their emergence: 'the Emergentists do not maintain that something is an emergent because it is unpredictable. Rather, they maintain that something can be unpredictable because it is an emergent. Emergence implies a kind of unpredictability. But it is a mistake to conflate emergence with this consequence of emergence. The British Emergentists do not' (McLaughlin 1992, 73).

importance of the latter problem can be seen, I believe, in Ellis and Murphy's discussion of a top-down effect. While such an effect is said to be consistent with microscopic laws and states determining macroscopic evolution, it nonetheless determines the detailed evolution of the system. How? The key notion is that of a *boundary condition*. Take, for instance, the position of the boundary on a container of gas. According to Ellis and Murphy it will 'determine the nature of the local molecular state of motion because it controls the pressure of the gas' (Ellis and Murphy 1996, 28). The reason why 'this is a case of a top-down effect' pertains to the fact that 'the concept of a boundary wall is a macroscopic concept, which does not make sense at a microscopic level,' that is, 'the very act of naming it a "boundary wall" invokes macroconcepts that are not part of the microvocabulary' (Ellis and Murphy 1996, 28).

It is crucially important to understand that while it is true that the concept of a 'boundary wall' is a different concept from what might be found in the microvocabulary, it does not follow for Ellis and Murphy that there is any robust top-down causation. *Semantic* and *epistemic* irreducibility do not entail *ontological* irreducibility.[37] Note that Ellis and Murphy grant that a 'particular macroscopic set of boundary conditions' are 'realized by a particular set of microscopic conditions.' If this is so, then there remain real micro-states upon which the macroscopic boundary conditions super-vene. When they claim that these microstates are 'not uniquely determined by the macrophysical state,' they are admitting only that a particular boundary condition is *multiply realizable* micro-physically. But none of this entails that the higher level *causally affects* the lower level; it only says that when we *think* the concept

---

[37] Imagine whole M as constituted by parts P_1 & P_2 & P_3, such that M has novel causal powers that are not merely the result of the interaction of the causal powers of P_1 v P_2 v P_3. (In other words, there is a 'more-thanness' to the causal powers of M.) In such a case, it seems a new property emerges in M such that there could be no identity between the set of M-properties and P-properties. Likewise, there cannot be an identity of facts. Could there be an identity of entities? It depends upon how one understands the property of having a causal power, and how one conceives the role of such properties in the individuation of entities. If events are individuated by spatio-temporal location, then one could perhaps talk about identity and concomitant *ontological reduction*.

at the higher level we do not (and cannot) *think* a particular micro-physical realization. Epistemic limitations do not permit bridge laws between macroscopic boundary conditions and their micro-physical realizations.[38]

In my opinion, what advocates of top-down causality want is for the higher level to make a real causal difference in actualizations at the lower level, a difference that exists apart from human awareness, concepts, and language. If God works in top-down fashion in the world, then that top-down causal relationship has temporally preceded any human awareness, concepts, or language. In other words, the top-down causation that eventuated in the evolution of human life is *real*. But if this is so, then how can God be understood as determinable by the lower-levels; how can he *be* an 'enveloping supervenient power'? (Nelson 1995, 280)

It must be recalled that supervenience theory is predominately used by philosophers attempting to articulate a *materialist* world view, and that these philosophers desire an explanation that is ultimately mechanistic in character. For them *teleological* explanation must be determined by, or somehow be dependent upon, *mechanistic* explanation. But the work that downward causation is supposed to do in the science–theology discussion is ultimately teleological. It is not clear that a supervenient reality of value, meaning, and purpose provides the ontological resources for a teleological, downward causation onto the physical.

The third problem concerns *mereological supervenience*, the relationship between the whole and its parts. Is such a super-venience committed to materialistic microreduction of the whole to the parts? While this is a controversial issue, it seems there are strong reasons to argue that it is so committed (Kim 1993, 101–2; Rowlands 1995). Even Trenton Merricks' recent argument against global microphysical supervenience – possible worlds qualitatively indiscernible at the microphysical level are qualitatively indis-cernible at the macrophysical level – admits that an object's

---

[38] Since there are no bridge laws *nomological reducibility* cannot obtain. However, *ontological reducibility* could still hold, and perhaps *causal reducibility* due to the *token identity* of the causal connections between events referred to by both higher and lower-level descriptions.

'intrinsic qualitative properties supervene on the features of, and restricted interrelations among, its constituent atoms' (Merricks 1998, 68).

Critically important to properly understanding the reductive proclivities of mereological supervenience is the distinction between *relational* and *nonrelational* properties. It is tempting to claim that the mental is realized neurophysiologically, but that it does *not* determinately supervene upon the neurophysiological, because different mental states can correlate with the same neurophysiological state (Putnam 1975; Burge 1979). While I have no space here to take up the issue, it is important to remember that mental states like 'seeing x' are essentially relational, i.e. their being depends upon the relation they sustain to their wider environment. But if this is so, then they cannot be expected to supervene on nonrelational neurophysiological states. However, if their subvenient physical base is expanded beyond brain states, there is no reason to think the mental state will fail determinately to supervene. In other words, if we are careful to keep both subvenient and supervenient properties nonrelational, or perhaps appropriately relational, it is extremely difficult to construct counter-examples to mereological supervenience – and its attendant reductionism.

Notice that all three of the problems we have discussed are really only difficulties for the post-Davidson conception of supervenience. Problem I is not an issue for emergentism, because God could, in principle, determine the universe's processes through top-down causation. Neither is II problematic, for emergentism thought that downward causation was thoroughly compatible with the bottom-up determination of emergents. Also problem III only arises in the post-Davidson discussion; for only this camp begins with the assumption that microphysical causality wholly determines higher-level causality.

It should be obvious from this essay that supervenience is a rather technical philosophical notion that admits of various formulations. I have tried both to highlight some of the important issues and distinctions within the supervenience literature, and to suggest ways in which the concept might be appropriated by those in the science–theology discussion. (I make no claims to completeness;

these are merely ways that have occurred to me.) Throughout, I have tried to point to some of the potential problems of using supervenience. I have suggested that two rather different senses of 'supervene' are historically distinguishable, and that one's advocacy of supervenience in the science–theology discussion will most likely be contingent upon which notion of supervenience is assumed. The British Emergentist concept of supervenience with its attendant *downward causation* should be more attractive to theologians than that employed in much of the post-Davidson discussion. Of course, one's advocacy of downward causation will ultimately depend upon one's evaluation of its coherence. I have suggested throughout this essay that the notion is deeply problematic. In my opinion, advocates of theological supervenience should concentrate their efforts on articulating a spirited defense of this concept. That the dominant position of contemporary analytic philosophy soundly rejects the notion should give proponents pause that such a defense can be successful.

References

ALEXANDER, SAMUEL. 1979. *Space, Time, and Deity*, 2 vols, Gloucester, MA: Peter Smith.

ARMSTRONG, DAVID. 1982. 'Metaphysics and Supervenience,' *Critica* 42:3–17.

———. 1989. *A Combinatorial Theory of Possibility*, Cambridge: Cambridge University Press.

BACON, JOHN. 1986. 'Supervenience, Necessary Coextension and Reducibility,' *Philosophical Studies* 49, 163–76.

BARBOUR, IAN. 1990. *Religion in an Age of Science*, San Francisco: Harper & Row.

BENDER, JOHN. 1987. 'Supervenience and the Justification of Aesthetic Judgments,' *Journal of Aesthetics and Art Criticism* 46, 31–40.

BIELFELDT, DENNIS. 1995. 'God, Physicalism, and Supervenience,' *Center for Theology and Natural Science Bulletin* 15, 1–12.

148   *Dennis Bielfeldt*

BIELFELDT, DENNIS. 1999. 'Supervenience as a Strategy for Relating Physical and Theological Properties,' in N. H. Gregersen, W. Drees, U. Görman and C. Wassermann (eds), *The Interplay Between Scientific and Theological Worldviews* I, Geneva: Labor et Fides, 161–76.

———. 2000. 'Is Christianity committed to Substance Dualism?,' *Zygon* (forthcoming).

BLACKBURN, SIMON. 1984. *Spreading the Word: Groundings in the Philosophy of Language*, Oxford: Oxford University Press.

BONEVAC, DANIEL. 1988. 'Supervenience and Ontology,' *American Philosophical Quarterly* 25, 35–47.

———. 1995. 'Reduction in the Mind of God,' in E. Savellos and Ü. Yalcin (eds), *Supervenience: New Essays*, Cambridge: Cambridge University Press, 124–39.

BURGE, TYLER. 1979. 'Individualism and the Mental,' in *Midwest Studies in Philosophy* 4, Minneapolis: University of Minnesota Press, 73–121.

CAMPBELL, D. T. 1974. '"Downward Causation" in Hierarchically Organized Biological Systems,' in F. Ayala and T. Dobzhansky (eds), *Studies in the Philosophy of Biology: Reduction and Related Problems*, Berkeley: University of California Press, 179–86.

CHALMERS, DAVID. 1996. *The Conscious Mind: In Search of a Fundamental Theory*, Oxford: Oxford University Press.

CURRIE, GREGORY. 1984. 'Individualism and Global Supervenience,' *British Journal of the Philosophy of Science* 35, 345–58.

———. 1990. 'Supervenience, Essentialism and Aesthetic Properties,' *Philosophical Studies* 58, 243–57.

DAVIDSON, DONALD. 1980. *Essays on Actions and Events*, Oxford: Clarendon Press.

———. 1993. 'Thinking Causes,' in A. Mele and J. Heil (eds), *Mental Causation*, Oxford: Clarendon Press, 3–17.

———. 1994. 'Donald Davidson,' in S. Guttenplan (ed.), *A Companion to the Philosophy of Mind*, Oxford: Blackwell, 231–6.

DREES, WILLEM. 1996. *Religion, Science and Naturalism*, Cambridge: Cambridge University Press.

ELLIS, GEORGE and MURPHY, NANCEY. 1996. *On the Moral Nature of the Universe: Theology, Cosmology, and Ethics*, Minneapolis: Fortress Press.

GREGERSEN, NIELS HENRIK. 1999. 'Divine Action in a Universe of Minds' (unpublished manuscript).

——. 2000. 'God's Public Traffic: Holist versus Physicalist Supervenience' (in this volume).

GRIMES, T. R. 1988. 'The Myth of Supervenience,' *Pacific Philosophical Quarterly* 69, 152–60.

GRIMES, T. R. 1995. 'The Tweedledum and Tweedledee of Supervenience,' in E. Savellos and Ü. Yalcin (eds), *Supervenience: New Essays*, 110–23.

HARE, R. 1952. *The Language of Morals*, Oxford: Clarendon Press.

——. 1984. 'Supervenience,' *The Aristotelian Society*, Supplementary 58, 1–16.

HAUGELAND, JOHN. 1982. 'Weak Supervenience,' *American Philosophical Quarterly* 19, 93–103.

HELLMAN, GEOFFRY. 1985. Determination and Logical Truth,' *Journal of Philosophy* 82, 607–16.

——. 1992. 'Supervenience/Determination a Two-Way Street? Yes, But One of the Ways is the Wrong Way!,' *Journal of Philosophy* 89, 42–7.

HELLMAN, G. AND THOMPSON, F. 1975. 'Physicalism: Ontology, Determination and Reduction,' *Journal of Philosophy* 72, 551–64.

HORGAN, TERRENCE. 1981. 'Token Physicalism, Supervenience, and the Generality of Physics,' *Syntheses* 49, 395–413.

——. 1982. 'Supervenience and Microphysics,' *Pacific Philosophical Quarterly* 63, 29–43.

——. 1993. 'From Supervenience to Superdupervenience: Meeting the Demands of the Material World,' *Mind* 102, 555–86.

HORGAN, TERRENCE. 1995. 'Reduction,' in J. Kim and E. Sosa (eds), *A Companion to Metaphysics*, Oxford: Blackwell, 438–40.

KIM, JAEGWON. 1985. 'Supervenience, Determination, and Reduction,' *Journal of Philosophy* 82, 616–18.

——. 1992. '"Downward Causation" in Emergentism and Nonreductive Physicalism,' in A. Beckermann, H. Flohr and J. Kim (eds), *Emergence or Reduction?*, Berlin: W. de Gruyter, 119–37.

——. 1993. *Supervenience and Mind*, Cambridge: Cambridge University Press.

——. 1994. 'Supervenience,' in S. Guttenplan (ed), *A Companion to the Philosophy of Mind*, Oxford: Blackwell, 575–83.

KLAGGE, JAMES. 1988. 'Supervenience: Ontological and Ascriptive,' *Australian Journal of Philosophy* 66, 461–70.

——. 1995. 'Supervenience: Model Theory or Metaphysics,' in E. Savellos and Ü. Yalcin (eds), *Supervenience: New Essays*, 60–72.

LEWIS, DAVID. 1986. *On the Plurality of Worlds*, Oxford: Blackwell.

MCLAUGLIN, BRIAN. 1984. 'Perception, Causation, and Supervenience,' in P. French, T. Uehling and H. Wettstein (eds), *Midwest Studies in Philosophy* 9, 569–91, Minneapolis: University of Minnesota Press.

——. 1992. 'The Rise and Fall of British Emergentism,' in A. Beckermann, H. Flor and J. Kim (eds), *Emergence or Reduction?*, Berlin: W. de Gruyter, 49–93.

——. 1995. 'Varieties of Supervenience,' in E. Savellos and Ü. Yalcin (eds), *Supervenience: New Essays* 16–59.

MELNYK, ANDREW. 1991. 'Physicalism: From Supervenience to Elimination,' *Philosophy and Phenomenological Research* 51, 573–87.

MERRICKS, TRENTON. 1998. 'Against the Doctrine of Microphysical Supervenience,' *Mind* 107, 60–71.

MILLER, RICHARD. 1990. 'Supervenience is a Two-Way Street,' *Journal of Philosophy* 87, 695–701.

MORGAN, LLOYD. 1926. *Emergent Evolution*, London: Williams & Norgate.

NELSON, JAMES. 1995. 'Divine Action: Is it Credible?' *Zygon* 30, 267–80.

PEACOCKE, ARTHUR. 1976. 'Reduction: A Review of the Epistemological Issues and their Relevance to Biology and the Problem of Consciousness,' *Zygon* 11, 307–31.

——. 1979. *Creation and the World of Science*, Oxford: Clarendon Press.

——. 1984. *Intimations of Reality*, Notre Dame: University of Notre Dame Press.

——. 1993. *Theology for a Scientific Age*, Minneapolis: Fortress Press.

PEPPER, STEPHEN. 1926. 'Emergence,' *Journal of Philosophy* 23, 241–5.

PETRIE, BRADFORD. 1987. 'Global Supervenience and Reduction,' *Philosophy and Phenomenological Research* 48, 119–30.

POST, J. 1984. 'Comments on Teller,' *Southern Journal of Philosophy* 22, Supplement, 163–7.

PUTNAM, HILARY. 1975. 'The Meaning of "Meaning",' in *Philosophical Papers*, vol. 2, Cambridge: Cambridge University Press.

ROWLANDS, MARK. 1995. *Supervenience and Materialism*, Aldershot, England: Avebury Press.

SAEGER, WILLIAM. 1988. 'Weak Supervenience and Materialism,' *Philosophy and Phenomenological Research* 48, 697–709.

SAVELLOS, ELIAS AND YALCIN, ÜMIT. 1995. 'Introduction,' in E. Savellos and Ü. Yalcin (eds), *Supervenience: New Essays*, Cambridge: Cambridge University Press, 1–15.

SEARLE, JOHN. 1992. *The Rediscovery of Mind*, Cambridge, Mass: MIT Press.

SOSA, ERNEST. 1984. 'Mind–Body Interaction and Supervenient Causation,' in P. French, T. Uehling and H. Wettstein (eds), *Midwestern Studies in Philosophy* 9, 271–81.

TELLER, PAUL. 1984a. 'A Poor Man's Guide to Supervenience and Determination,' *Southern Journal of Philosophy* 22, 137–67.

TELLER, PAUL. 1984b. 'Comment on Kim's Paper,' *Southern Journal of Philosophy* 22, Supplement, 57–62.

——. 1992. 'A Contemporary Look at Emergence,' in H. Flohr and J. Kim (eds), *Emergence or Reduction?*, Berlin: W. de Gruyter, 139–53.

——. 1995. 'Supervenience,' in J. Kim and E. Sosa (eds), *A Companion to Metaphysics*, Oxford: Blackwell, 484–6.

VAN CLEVE, JAMES. 1990. 'Supervenience and Closure,' *Philosophical Studies* 58, 225–38.

8

God's Public Traffic: Holist versus Physicalist Supervenience

NIELS HENRIK GREGERSEN

Introduction

In the present essay I wish to correlate two strands of thought which belong to different traditions and are usually regarded as incompatible. One framework is philosophical in nature and concerns the link between brain and mind. According to supervenience theories, mental processes are 'supervenient' upon their 'subvenient base' in the physical structure of the human brain. Thus, there are differences between mental and physical properties, but since the functioning of the mind depends on the brain there cannot exist any separate human mind.

The other strand of thought relates to the theology of the sacraments. According to Martin Luther's eucharistic theology, God is effectively present in, with and under publicly available signs such as words, water, wine and bread. Furthermore, God is assumed to use the Lord's Supper for the purpose of divine self-communication and human transformation so that a transition from greed to love can take place in the mind of the believer.

How could we constructively develop such a high theological claim in relation to contemporary philosophy of mind? How can we think of God's transformative presence in the minds of believers on the basis of a non-dualist account, that is, an account which presupposes (1) that the brain has priority over the mind, and (2) that mental properties remain dependent upon their natural and social embodiments? My purpose is to demonstrate that a 'thick' theological notion of divine action (that is, a notion developed on the basis of Christian self-understanding) is perfectly intelligible within the boundaries of a supervenience theory. Particularly, I shall emphasize that eucharistic theology offers a model for understanding how so-called 'special divine action' is always mediated through the interplay of physical substructure, mental apprehensions and socially shared meanings. The eucharistic triad of (1) material elements, (2) apprehensible signs and words and (3) a particular social setting may illuminate how the human person is theologically defined both by his or her roots in nature and by his or her relations to God and other persons.

What kind of correlation could possibly be achieved between a eucharistic theology and a philosophy of mind? Let it be clear from the outset that I am not pursuing an inductive apologetic argument pretending that the presence of God can be evidenced or otherwise inferred from a philosophy of mind. The kind of theology to be presented here is not a piece of natural theology. Rather, a line of reasoning is developed which allows for a resonance between a historically given belief system, in my case a Reformation theology of the Eucharist, and a specific version of supervenience theory.

Elsewhere I have laid out a *contextual coherence theory* for the science–theology dialogue (Gregersen 1998a). By 'coherence' I here mean that a eucharistic theology about God's transformation of human minds through external words and signs can be articulated within the framework of a non-dualist theory of mind. 'Contextual' qualifies the kind of coherence to be searched for. Assuming that the overall texture of human knowledge entails a plurality of irreducible perspectives we should acknowledge that modes of thought belonging to different contexts of inquiry cannot be homogenized, or otherwise synthesized, without a substantial loss of meaning. Thus, a theological perspective on the human self is neither empirically inferred from nor logically implied by a certain philosophical perspective. Though religious beliefs remain sensitive to changes in world-view and mindset, religious practices make up a relatively independent context of meaning.

Modes of thought are often not connected by rigid logic, or by formal or informal inference. The contextual coherence theory makes the weaker claim that *if* non-theological assumptions of reality are changed, *then* the truth claims of theology would not be unaffected. If, for instance, a *mind–body dualism* would turn out to be philosophically preferable, the interest in the interface between theology and science would probably diminish; also a sacramental theology would be of secondary concern, since God could immediately communicate Godself to an individual soul through a purely spiritual medium (e.g. an 'inner voice'). On the other hand, if a *reductionist physicalism* were to prevail in the philosophy of mind, the human person would be seen as nothing but a surface reality, an epiphenomenal expression of a pack of molecules (Nyborg 1997). Accordingly, theology would face the stark choice of either reducing all theological statements into a theory of bottom-up divine determinism, or maintaining theology as an inquiry dissociated from contemporary scientific models of reality. Fortunately, however, theology does not seem to be in such a difficult position.

Two Versions of Supervenience

In the current science–theology discussion, the idea of supervenience has been used as an attractive way to steer a middle path between the Scylla of a radical mind–body dualism and the Charybdis of a reductive physicalism. Mental properties emerge on the basis of physical properties, but once mental features are stabilized they may exercise a 'downwards' causal role within physical reality. Within the framework of a more general emergentist world-view, supervenience seems to suggest the viability of a *non-reductive physicalism*.[1] Furthermore, the term 'supervening'

---

[1] Following the work of Donald T. Campbell and Roger W. Sperry on downwards causation, Arthur Peacocke developed a ground-breaking level theory for understanding the interrelation between the biological, the psychological and the social levels of human personhood, summarized in Peacocke 1993, esp.

differs in an interesting way from that of 'intervening.' While an intervention suggests that something new is coming into play from the outside, supervenience refers to occurrences that are coming up *from within* a given setting. Could perhaps the concept of supervenience also help us finding a *via media* between an interventionist model of divine action and a deistic notion of an inert God?

In common usage 'supervene' is a rare word, but it can be used in sayings such as 'difficulties supervened,' or 'a storm supervened.' The term itself suggests the addition of something unexpected occurring within certain circumstances. In this vein, *Webster's Encyclopedic Unabridged Dictionary of the English Language* (1994) renders the term *supervening* as 'taking place or occurring as something additional or extraneous.' Thus, the expression of real *novelty* seems to be part of the lexical meaning.

Against this background evolutionary emergentists like C. Lloyd Morgan, C. D. Broad, or Samuel Alexander embraced the term supervenience and coined it into a philosophical concept. The general idea of emergentism is that new holistic properties always appear on the basis of certain constellations of physical chemistry, but once they are formed, these emergent properties can no longer be described on the basis of the constituent parts of that system, nor can their behavior be predicted without taking the system as a whole into account. In the words of Samuel Alexander,

---

pp. 213–54. While introducing the theory of supervenience, the level theory was later expanded by Nancey Murphy and George F. R. Ellis (1996, 19–38; cf. Murphy 1997, 193–208), by Philip Clayton (1997, 247–57) and programmatically in Warren S. Brown, Nancey Murphy and H. Newton Malony, eds (1998). Dennis Bielfeldt has probably made the most detailed analyses of the concept of supervenience in the science–theology debate. In an early proposal he suggests that divine action might be understood as a quality supervening on the material substructure of the universe (Bielfeldt 1995). On this view, however, divine action is ontologically dependent upon the physical processes, rather than the other way around. Even if Bielfeldt carefully argues that supervenience could thus only account for God's immanent workings, it still appears that this early proposal only baptizes the spin-offs of brain processes as 'divine properties.' Later, Bielfeldt has expressed more reser-vations as to the potentials of the supervenience theory for theology (see Bielfeldt 1999 and 2000 (in this volume)).

The higher quality emerges from the lower level of existence and has its roots therein, but it emerges therefrom, and it does not belong to that level, but constitutes its possessor a new order of existent with its special laws of behaviour. The existence of emergent qualities thus described is something to be noted, as some would say, under the compulsion of brute empirical fact, or, as I should prefer to say in less harsh terms, to be accepted with the 'natural piety' of the investigator. It admits no explanation. (Alexander 1920, II.46f.)

Notice that according to this definition not all supervenient properties would be counted as emergent properties. Higher-level emergents seem to be one distinct class of supervenient properties among others (O'Connor 1994, 98). Alexander distinguishes *emergent* phenomena from mere *resultant* phenomena (Alexander 1920, II.14). The first (but not the latter) inaugurate a new series of qualities and behaviors which can no longer be explained from the physical base that caused their emergence in the first place. Think of the difference between minds and tables. Whereas the phenomenological properties of the solidity of tables are mere *resultants* of the physical structure (since the solidity of tables does not change their chemical basis), mind is an *emergent* new quality of neural life that begins to lead a life of its own and may end up having a feedback influence on the subvenient structures of the brain. In this way, the general idea of supervenience was well suited to push the twofold aim of the emergentists by ensuring the possibility of *real novelty* in emergent phenomena of life, while affirming their *material* base in the ordinary biochemistry of matter. So far the employment of the concept of supervenience by the evolutionary emergentists was backed up by the pre-philosophical usage of the term.[2]

However, the route from supervenience to emergentist downward causation might not be as direct as often assumed. Dennis Bielfeldt (1999; 2000) has argued that the employment of supervenience theory in recent science–theology discussion is at variance

---

[2] It is hardly correct to say that there is 'no pre-existing concept [of supervenience] to be analyzed' (Kim 1995, 133), before it was coined as a philosophical concept. After all, there seems to be some reliable linguistic intuitions to guide our understanding of the way from the pre-philosophic to the philosophical use of the term.

with the general idea of supervenience in today's analytical philosophy of mind. Though the term 'supervenience' came up in the 1920s with the British emergentists (most of whom believed in top-down causality), Bielfeldt finds that supervenience in current analytical philosophy of mind presupposes a causal closure of the physical world which strictly denies the possibility of downward causality. I agree with Bielfedt that the concept of supervenience is far from unambiguous. Rather than embracing a generic understanding of supervenience, we need to disentangle different versions of supervenience and different versions of non-reductive physicalism.

In the following I wish to explicate the differences between Jaegwon Kim's physicalist and Donald Davidson's holist versions of supervenience. My own reasons for opting for the latter will then be developed through Karl Popper's level theory of the three interacting worlds, World 1 of physical facts, World 2 of mental facts, and World 3 of cultural facts. Whereas physicalist supervenience denies downwards causation, holist supervenience theory has some affinity with a level theory (though the latter is not entailed in the former). My main argument in favor of mental causation is that the mental properties of an individual human person are connected to wider social networks of meaning (including particular language systems) which definitely transcend the individual brain. Since one cannot understand the states of consciousness of an individual apart from his or her relatedness to this wider semantic context, it is, by definition, not possible to reduce mental states to the physical states of a brain.

In a later section, I will develop some main ideas in Martin Luther's eucharistic theology. The pivotal point here is that God's action in the world is assumed to take place in the context of publicly available signs and meanings, in a top-down manner, and should not be seen as something going on behind the back of human persons. This theological interpretation is coherent with the holist supervenience but is in conflict with physicalist supervenience. In the present context, I am not engaged in a critical reconstruction of the theology of the sacraments but I hope to illuminate how and why theological tradition emphasizes that

God's interaction with human beings takes place in the public sphere of words, signs and social settings.

Two Forms of Non-Reductionism, Two Theories of Supervenience

Jaegwon Kim's influential version of supervenience contends that mental properties are causally inert *qua* mental since only the physical bases are causally effective. Kim is a proponent of what I shall here call the *physicalist version of supervenience*. Against this background, I suggest a distinction between two versions of non-reductive physicalism:

> *Non-reductive physicalism1* (semantic non-reductionism):
> Mental states cannot *definitionally* be reduced to brain states
>
> *Non-reductive physicalism2* (causal non-reductionism):
> Mental states cannot be *nomologically* reduced to brain states.

A physicalist supervenience theorist like Jaegwon Kim is a proponent of a non-reductive physicalism1, since he endorses the view that mental features cannot be described as physical properties. The description 'I feel a sudden pain,' cannot be *semantically* reduced to a physiological description of neurological changes of brain states. Being a physicalist supervenience theorist, however, Kim rejects non-reductive physicalism2, since he rejects the view that mental states can do any causal job in addition to or distinct from that neurological events. Any mental state is *causally* determined by brain states. Opting for a microphysical determinism, Kim also believes that there exist strict psychophysical laws determining the mental resultants of the brain's activity. The supervenient states of the mind can be *nomologically* reduced to their subvenient brain states.

As rightly pointed out by Dennis Bielfeldt in this volume, it is inconsistent to argue for top-down mental causation and quote Kim in support of this view. In contrast to Bielfeldt, however, I would argue that downward mental causation gives a more convincing account of the brain–mind relation than does the physicalist version of supervenience. There is another version of supervenience in analytical philosophy of mind which I shall dub *holist supervenience*. This version of supervenience adopts the stance of a non-reductionism2 and affirms the causal efficacy of mind.

The holist version of supervenience is associated with the name of Donald Davidson. On his account, mental causation is not excluded by supervenience. Supervenience certainly implies a kind of brain–mind monism, but neither a definitional nor a nomological reduction of mental properties.[3]

To believe that a mental event is causally inert is not only counter-intuitive, it also seems to compromise the basic assumption of supervenience theory that mental events are always *also* physical events. Mental and physical properties form a *unity*. Thus, supervenience implies some kind of *dual-aspect monism* but it does not imply a physicalist reductionism which holds that an explanation in terms of fundamental physics is under all circumstances and about any object privileged to explanations in terms of intentions, actions, etc. Jaegwon Kim's claim that mental events are only efficacious *qua* physical – not *qua* mental – presupposes an additional metaphysical assumption, namely that physics is all that matters in causal connections.

According to Davidson, the physicalist supervenience theorist disregards the encompassing unity of mental and physical. Certainly, there is a *type-difference* between the mental and the physical, but since there is *no ontological separation*, there is no need to regard purely physical explanations as complete. Causal schemes covering mental and physical aspects of the one and same event are preferable to one monolithic explanatory scheme which only covers an event's microphysical substructure. Since any particular mental event can only be understood against the background of a wider set of culturally shared beliefs, mental events display holist features that are not accountable under physical descriptions. Thus we may formulate the two versions of supervenience as follows:

---

[3] Davidson (1995, 5): 'supervenience in any form implies monism; but it does not imply either definitional or nomological reduction.'

Supervenience Theory1 (physicalist supervenience theory):
Mental states (always based on physical states) cannot adequately be described in physicalist language, though they are causally determined by micro-physical states

Supervenience Theory2 (holist supervenience theory):
Mental states (always based on physical states) can neither adequately be described in physicalist language nor be nomologically reduced to physical states.

As appears from the latter definition, holist supervenience theory retains the priority of the physical substructure of reality in so far as mental aspects of reality could not exist nor be sustained without their physical bases. In contrast to physicalism, however, holistic supervenience theory supports a *neutral monism*, that is, the doctrine that all of reality ultimately forms a unity which can neither be described nor be sufficiently explained in either physical or mental terms.[4]

Donald Davidson's 'Anomalous Monism'

In his influential article 'Mental Events' of 1970, Davidson's starting point is a 'monism' which holds that all events have a physical substructure. Ontologically, there are *no events* which are not physical; all mental events are *also* physical events. However, there are *properties* of the mental that cannot be described in terms of physics (Davidson 1980, 214).

Davidson's monism is furthermore qualified with 'anomalous.' There is some irregularity with the mental. *Nomos* means law, and the a-nomaly of the mental means that mental features do not fall

---

[4] Even if Davidson does not explicitly use the term 'neutral monism,' I believe his position can best be described as such; cf. his interpreter Simon Evnine (1991, 64): 'Underlying the argument for anomalous monism is the idea that events, in themselves, are neither physical nor mental. What makes an event a mental, or physical, event, is whether or not it has a mental, or physical, description. Davidson's choice of the term "monism", rather than, say, "materialism" [or physicalism, (NHG)], to describe his theory, is a good one. What is important is not so much that all events are physical as that events form a single, and ontologically, neutral, class of entities.' On the concept of 'neutral monism,' see McLaughlin (1995, 599).

under strict physical laws. Consequently, there cannot exist general psychophysical laws by which one could translate mental properties into physical, and vice versa. Even if we may be able to explain causally a specific mental event (e.g. a pain) on the basis of a definite physical pattern of events (a hammer striking a thumb + the intricate causal routes within the nervous system), we could not formulate general psychophysical laws (brain processes like type x determine mental process like type y). There may be a *token–token identity*, but not a *type–type identity* by which one could translate physical properties into mental ones.

Davidson's original insight is exactly that particular events (the token–token identities) are more fundamental than our grand metaphysical assumptions about the causal cement between general types of properties. Just because one and the same thing can be both 'a piece of silk' and a 'tie,' one should not infer that silk in general is identical with the species of ties, or that all kinds of ties are made of silk. Again, even if a 'tie' can also be 'a birthday present,' we would not think that all ties are birthday presents and that all birthday presents consist of ties. There may be a token–token identity between a given portion of the material structure of silk and a particular birthday present, but it is impossible to state a type–type identity between physical and mental properties. Psychophysical laws which universally connect physical and mental properties are philosopher's daydreams.

Fundamental to Davidsons's differentiation between tokens and types is his thesis that we should carefully distinguish between *causal events*, which are always singular in nature, and *causal explanations*, which consist of more general descriptive schemes (1980, 215). As a monist Davidson presupposes that any event is ultimately physical in nature (any birthday present is made of something); furthermore, from brute experience we know that some events have *also* mental properties (such as 'a present for your birthday').

The pivotal question is, of course, whether mental properties such as 'being a gift' can be sufficiently explained on their physical bases alone. This depends upon what we mean by 'sufficiently explained.' In an article on 'Causal Relations' from 1967 Davidson gives the example, 'Brutus's stab was sufficient for Caesars's death.'

As we know from our history books, Caesar's death was the death of a man with more wounds than Brutus inflicted (1980, 157). Already on the physical level of description, the event picked out for explanation may only be part of the cause. Brutus's stab was a sufficient cause, but not the whole cause. Moreover, a variety of mental descriptions would be required if we would want to explain Caesar's death more fully – for example, why it came to the fatal event that Brutus and his followers stabbed Caesar. An event may have many or few causes. Under all circumstances, however, our causal explanations pick out the relevant ones for a given problem in question, in this case 'How and why did Caesar die?' *The event is one but the causal schemes are many.* According to Davidson, there is no important sense in which psychology can be reduced to the physical sciences. If we by 'science' mean a study of strict laws, there is no hope for establishing psychology as science (1980, 249).

Davidson, however, is by no means a relativist. Being a monist he has no interest in downplaying the relevance of neuroscience and biology for the study of psychological phenomena. Because of the token–token identity, he affirms that *this* particular brain event is covariant with *that* mental event. An explanation of human behavior in terms of neurological processes would make reference to the specific areas of the brain which are causally important for this or that mental phenomenon.[5] For example the hippocampus

---

[5] In personal communication (Iceland, July 1999), Nancey Murphy has questioned my use of causal language about the supervenience relation. According to Murphy, supervenience relations would be better defined as having 'non-causal consequences.' Murphy's concern is here to avoid the misconception that we have two discrete events (a physical event + a mental event); what we have, in fact, is one event with both mental and a physical descriptions. On this latter issue I agree with Murphy (see note 4 on 'neutral monism'). However, I do not see why one should restrict a causal language to discrete events (after all, what is ontologically discrete in nature?). In my view, the supervenience relation is a prime example of a *self-causation* (or *autopoiesis*). Given the right environment, the neuronal system produces first-hand consciousness and even social communication, which, once emerged, will have a feedback effect on future brain states by way of selective emphasis. Playing the violin, speaking a language, performing mathematical calcualtions, making love – all this structures the brain by carving out preferred routes of energy exchange in the brain system. This is a case of what philosopher Fred Dretske has helpfully termed a 'structuring causality' (cf. Gregersen 1998, 358–61).

and the amygdala are known to affect *declarative memories* such as remembering and naming events and persons, whereas *procedural memories* about how to do things seems to be caused by more ancient parts of the brain. Such a localizationist view of the brain and its causal effects is well documented in neuropsychological research. Davidson has no objections against token–token enquiries, nor does he have any quarrels with 'rough correlations' (1980, 231) between types of psychological and types of physical phenomena such as the correlations between memory and brain parts indicated above. Davidson maintains, however, that general correlations could never be turned into a strict law connecting brains and minds (1980, 250). Even if we were in the possession of a complete knowledge of the physics of a human being, this knowledge would not suffice to pick out the important classes of events which are defined by psychological predicates. There is no general law connecting the statement 'This is a bundle of silk,' with the statement, 'This tie is a birthday present for you.'

'[M]ental and physical predicates are not made for one another' (Davidson 1980, 218). In the terminology of W. V. Quine, there is an Indeterminacy of Translation involved here, because the commitments and perspectives of physical and mental explanations cannot be unified. We simply end up in a mishmash if we try to look for bridging laws between incompatible descriptions:

> There are no strict psychophysical laws because of the disparate commitments of the mental and physical schemes. It is a feature of physical reality that physical change can be explained by laws that connect it with other changes and conditions physically described. It is a feature of the mental that the attribution of mental phenomena must be responsible to the background of reasons, beliefs, and intentions of the individual. There cannot be tight connections between the realms if each is to retain allegiance to its proper source of evidence. (1980, 222)

Mental events are internally correlated so as to meet a variety of *rational* conditions, such as coherence and consistency.

The Holism of the Mental

Why this insistence on the *type-difference* between mental and physical descriptions? The main reason is, as we shall see, that the mental makes up a cognitive field which is *holistic* in nature and entails a variety of *normative* features, and these features 'have no echo in physical theory' (1980, 231).

The holist and normative character of the mental can be inferred from the example of mathematics. The occurrence of some specific neuronal events in my brain may be accompanied by my conducting a mathematical calculation like, for instance, 'If $5+3 = 8$, then $50+30$ is necessarily 80.' According to Davidson, one might rightly say that a given neuronal pattern was the cause of this particular mental operation. However, does the physical structure of the brain offer the complete and exclusive explanation of this calculation? After all, it seems that mental operations such as 'calculating' make up a logical realm of their own. It cannot be that my calculations rely exclusively on the specific brain states that I happen to occupy today, nor on my general moods. Whether at present I am in this or that brain state, whether I am happy or gloomy, whether I have been raised in Tehran or in Beijing, I can still perform the mathematical argument 'If $5+3 = 8$, then $50+30$ is necessarily 80.' Two things are important here. First, being a natural number is a *holistic* property, since numbers are defined by their successor relations; one does not understand what '30' means unless one understands the number system as a whole. Second, there is in this case an irredeemable *normativity* built into mental operations, since one could not escape the conclusion that 'If $50+30 = 80$, then $500+300$ is *necessarily* 800.' Again, there is no direct echo of the modal operator 'necessarily' in our complex neuronal firings. It is only within the mathematical argument that it can be determined whether a given relation is purely accidental, is empirically necessary, or is cogent by logical implication. This primitive example shows why mental operations are not purely a *result* of certain brain processes but make up an *emergent* reality with its own logical standards. Mathematics implies a *logical holism*. Furthermore the example demonstrates the extent to which the normative rules of the mental are clearly *extrinsic* to the individual holder of a brain, since the rules open up a whole space of other convictions (in this case mathematical in kind).

Informal languages are not less holistic than mathematics: like mathematics, they are extrinsic to the individual person's brain.[6] The additional difficulty is that informal languages (like Hebrew, Chinese, Zulu, and Danish) are bound to historically developed cultural horizons. The holism of the mental is here a *semantic holism*. One cannot be 'married' unless one is married to another person, who is, by definition, married to oneself; one cannot be a 'son' without having parents, etc. In short, languages depend upon *relational properties* that are no longer intrinsic to the individual brain. Furthermore, it makes a difference to refer to 'my wife' in a monogamous culture and in a polygamous culture; a number of further differences would obtain if we were to understand the meaning of a single utterance like 'This is my wife' in a Chinese, a Zulu, or in a Danish culture. As phrased by Davidson, 'Only in the context of the language does a sentence (and therefore a word) have meaning' (1984, 22).

Part of *explaining* a speech act means *interpreting* it on the basis of the speaker's language, that is, on the basis of that person's culturally shaped expectations and the array of semantic possibilities afforded by a given language.

> To interpret a single speech act, therefore, we must have a grasp of the speaker's unrealized dispositions to perform other speech acts ... We describe the disposition by specifying what the speaker would mean by uttering any of a large number of sentences under specified conditions. (1980, 255)

Understanding a mental event is thus by definition an open-ended inquiry which could never be explained within a deterministic law-like framework. To understand an utterance means to understand the web of background assumptions and potentialities of any speaker. So far, Davidson shares Quine's concept of meaning holism which holds that any singular meaning is part of a 'web of beliefs.' Just as Quine speaks about the Indeterminacy of Translation involved in the connection of one sentence to other sentences, Davidson speaks of *Radical Interpretation*. However, unlike Quine

---

[6] On the varieties of holisms, especially semantic holism, see the instructive geography of issues in Jerry Fodor and Ernest Lepore (1993, 1–35).

(who is a behaviorist), Davidson thinks that the way of understanding an utterance is always by way of *redescription*, that is, by
replacing one utterance with another in one's own vocabulary in
order to grasp in a conjectural way what the contents of other
persons' dispositions and propositions may be. There is no direct
way to check one's interpretation by the external behavior of others.
We are always forced into an ongoing learning-process of redescription:

> The task may be seen as one of redescription. We know that the words
> 'Es schneit' have been uttered on a particular occasion and we want to
> redescribe this uttering as an act of saying that it is snowing. (1984,
> 141)

Supervenience Revisited

From this general perspective of anomalous monism and mental
holism, let us return to the different versions of supervenience.

In analytical philosophy (as distinct from the tradition of the
emergentists), the concept of supervenience was first used with
respect to ethical and aesthetical properties. Already in 1922 G. E.
Moore held that evaluative properties could not be reduced to
descriptive properties; however, the descriptive properties are
primary in relation to the evaluative properties so that two things
could not be exactly identical in descriptive properties and yet
differ in some evaluative property such as 'good' or 'beautiful.'
Later, R. M. Hare in *The Language of Morals* (1952) argued that if
one says 'St Francis was a good man,' it is illogical to make such a
statement and at the same time maintain that another person,
behaving like St Francis under exactly the same circumstances, is
not a good man. Supervenience applied to morality means

> the doctrine that moral judgments made about one situation, etc., have,
> on pain of logical inconsistency, to be made about any situation
> which is exactly similar in its universal non-moral properties. (Hare
> 1990, 268)

Notice that this definition of supervenience is both narrower and
broader than its use in Davidson's philosophy of mind. It is
narrower, since it only relates to moral descriptions and not to all
kinds of mental operations, like counting numbers, feeling an ache,

seeing television, or believing in God. It is broader, however, in so far as the supervenience relation is between evaluative properties and the physical circumstances beyond the human body and its brain. By contrast, when Donald Davidson in 1970 introduced the notion of supervenience into the philosophy of mind, his point was only to state a dependence relation between mental features and features of the physical brain. Anyway, it is clear that the very idea of supervenience implies a *correlation* between mental and physical aspects of reality, and also that the physical retains some priority in relation to the mental.

> [T]here cannot be two events alike in all physical respects but differ-
> ing in some mental respect, or that an object cannot alter in some
> mental respect without altering in some physical respect. (Davidson
> 1980, 214)

Supervenience may fall short of bridging psychophysical laws, but the notion of supervenience certainly represents a tightening of the relation between mental and physical properties compared to anomalous monism (Evnine 1991, 68). The question is, How tight?

First, supervenience allows for the *asymmetry* that numerous physical states may correlate to the same mental state. For example, our perception of colors can emerge on the basis of the different wavelengths of light, as we know from Newton's *Optics*. But color vision can also arise as an effect of different intensities of light beams, all of them having the same wavelength (the so-called *Bezold-Brücke* effect used in television technology). This Principle of Multiple Realization also applies to the relation between mental events and the internal functions of the brain. One and the same proposition ('this chair is blue') can be held as true by many different persons and can be realized in a variety of brain states of the same person.

Let us now revert to Jaegwon Kim's physicalist supervenience theory. Kim endorses Davidson's Principle of Multiple Realiza-tion. But he regards Davidson's 'anomalous monism' as unstable. On Kim's interpretation of Davidson, anomalous monism 'permits mental properties no causal role, not even in relation to other mental properties.' Rather than giving us a non-reductive physicalism, Davidson is said essentially to end up in 'a form of eliminativism' which allows mentality to exist, but its occurrence is left 'wholly mysterious and causally inexplicable' (Kim 1995a, 270).

It is against this interpretation that Davidson strongly protests in his response to Kim (Davidson 1995). Being a proponent of 'neutral monism,' Davidson is not willing to give privilege to purely physical explanations over against mental explanations. Perhaps one could say that Davidson's original version was a *semantic supervenience theory*, since he initially only argued for the impossibility of a translation between physical and mental properties while bracketing the question of the causal power of the mental. In his response to Kim, however, Davidson has reaffirmed the import of mental descriptions by referring to intentions and actions:

> [I]f mental concepts are not reducible to physical concepts, there is no reason to suppose we would lose interest in explanation in mental terms just because we had a complete physical explanation. (1995,16)[7]

Though Kim, in his reply to Davidson, concedes that the idea of anomalous monism does not logically entail a causal inertness of the mental, he maintains his earlier point that Davidson has failed to provide a positive explanation for the causal efficacy of mental properties (Kim 1995b, 20). In order to forestall an elimination of the mental Kim opts for an epiphenomenalism according to which mental properties can be counted as 'real' (from a phenomenological perspective) though causally inert. In this picture, all causal relations involving observable phenomena familiar to us from daily existence are 'cases of epiphenomenal causation' (Kim 1995a, 95). The supervenient properties of mind are *completely* determined by their supervenience bases in the form of a number of physically distinct microproperties (1995a, 98):

> (1) When mental event M causes another mental event M*, this is so because M supervenes on a physical state P, and similarly M* on P*, and P causes P*.

---

[7] Cf. the explanatory role attached to reason in explaining actions already in Davidson (1980, 12–19), and his later insistence that his concept of supervenience, though it implies a monism, does not imply a causal inertness of the mental in terms of epiphenomenalism (Davidson 1995, 5 and 12 ff.).

(2) When a mental event M causes a physical event P, this is because M is supervenient upon a physical event, P*, and P* causes P. (cf. Kim 1995a, 106)

Kim's position can be visualized as in Figure 1. Kim's micro-deterministic position entails a so-called *mereological* supervenience relation, that is, all supervenient properties in the system as a whole are strictly determined by and reducible to their parts (Greek *meros* = part).[8] On Kim's account, one could not make any distinction between emergents and resultants. Just as a given amount of H_2Os under appropriate temperature appears as water, so do brain processes result in psychological properties.

FIGURE 1: A MODEL OF A PHYSICALIST SUPERVENIENCE THEORY

$$M_1 \rightarrow M_2 \rightarrow M_3$$

$$\Uparrow \qquad \Uparrow \qquad \Uparrow$$

$$B_1 \Rightarrow B_2 \Rightarrow B_3 \dots.$$

B denotes brain states as the subvenient bases of mental states. B $\Rightarrow$ denotes efficient causation; M $\rightarrow$ epiphenomenal causation.

By contrast, holist supervenience theorists do not believe that the whole is determined by its constituent parts. It is not possible to account for, say, the necessity of mathematical logic by reference to ever-changing neuronal states. Since there is 'no echo' of the holistic and normative properties of the mental in the properties of atoms and quarks, mereological supervenience is not a plausible hypothesis: at least, there is no evidence to back it up.

---

[8] Cf. Kim (1995a, 101): 'Mereological supervenience is usefully taken to be a general thesis affirming the supervenience of the characteristics of wholes on the properties and relationships characterizing their parts ... Mereological supervenience (...) requires that each macrocharacteristic be grounded in some specific microcharacteristics.'

The question remains, however, whether a holist supervenience theory is able to corroborate its thesis of real mental causation? Recall that Kim concedes that Davidson's anomalous monism does not imply a denial of mental causation, while adding that Davidson has failed to make a positive case for the causal efficacy of the mental (Kim 1995b, 20f.). With Kim, I believe that Davidson's insistence on the semantical difference between mental and physical descriptions (on the epistemological level) is not in itself a conclusive evidence for a causal efficacy of the mental (on the ontological level). However, Davidson has given us compelling reasons why a physicalist determinism is bound to fail. Moreover, I believe that the positive case for mental causation can be strengthened, if we add to Davidson a more elaborated level theory. What follows is a sketch of such a metaphysical argument in support of a holist supervenience theory. The continued existence of consciousness depends on biology, but is nonetheless efficacious in its operations.

The Invalidity of Local Supervenience, the Vacuity of Global Supervenience

Let me begin by proposing a distinction between first-order and second-order states of consciousness (cf. Edelman 1992, 111–23). Primary consciousness consists of states in which we are mentally aware of something around us or in ourselves such as immediately feeling an ache or sensing an object in our surroundings. Second-order consciousness, by contrast, presuppose an interdependence between immediate impressions like these and a socially shared language. Only on this level do we find a mental holism with features such as counting, giving ties as birthday presents, and reportable states of self-reflection.

Kim and Davidson agree that a unilateral account from brain to mind may be possible with respect to primary consciousness. Such determination is well documented by neuroscience as well as supported by common sense. One can expect that future neuroscience will give further evidence for such token–token dependencies. Strong reasons, however, speak against a physical determinism with respect to higher-order consciousness. As soon as this level of consciousness is attained, the consciousness of an individual can no longer be explained without including properties that emerge only in the context of a co-evolution of mind and culture. For example, the extraordinary excitement among human beings about a bundle of a small green pieces of paper can only be explained by understanding it as 'a bundle of hundred-dollar bills.' In other words, it is not the *intrinsic physical properties* of bills that make the difference, but their *observer-relative properties*, and these observer-relative properties require an explanation in terms of mind and social structures. 'Hundred-dollar bills' are objective facts of our world, and constitute a new fact that transcends the fact of there being a heap of green paper pieces.[9] At one and the same time, 'hundred-dollar bills' belong to the physical system (by being made of paper), to the mental system (by being noticed by an apprehending subject) and to the social system (by being 'counted' as a means for exchanging values). It may be true that a brain causes mind, and that the development of brains is a *sufficient* explanation of the emergence of mind. However, the physical functioning of brain is not the *complete* explanation of *what* mind is, *how* it works, what it *effects*.[10]

This brings us back to the basic assumption of brain–mind supervenience that if two neuronal patterns were exactly identical, the same mental operation would occur. The question is now, How far does this principle leads us in front of the empirical fact that brains are extremely different? The answer will of course depend upon what we mean by 'physical sameness.' It would appear that the conditions for 'sameness' are extremely difficult to account for empirically. After all, is it possible for two things to be 'exactly the same' without occupying the same location and thus being placed in exactly the same circumstances? Probably not.

Nancey Murphy has offered a compelling argument as to why evaluative properties like 'St Francis is a good man' cannot be

---

[9] See John R. Searle's theory of institutional facts (1995, 1–13) and John Teske's (2000) contribution to this volume.

[10] In Gregersen (1998b, 335–40) I have further developed the idea of type-different causality within the theory of autopoietic systems.

extended to other persons, so that one could say that just any other person who is behaving like St Francis and having the same motivations as he has, must by definition also be a good person. According to Murphy,

> it is conceivable that identical behavior in different circumstances would *not* constitute goodness. For example, we would evaluate Francis's life much differently if he had been married and the father of children. (Murphy 1998, 134)

The example shows that moral properties do not supervene locally on particular brain states. Recall that Hare carefully argued that any other man being 'exactly similar in its universal non-moral properties' as St Francis would also have same moral properties (Hare 1990, 268). Certainly, this thought experiment of global supervenience holds true, but it is a truism, since two persons placed under the *exactly the same* circumstances would not be two persons but one person! Whether one defines the individuation of events by its occupying the same spatio-temporal location (so Quine, and the later Davidson), or by their unique role in causal patterns (so the early Davidson), 'sameness in all physical respects' would imply a strict identity.[11]

Thus it seems that *while physicalist local supervenience is wrong, physicalist global supervenience leads us nowhere in determining particular brain–mind relations.* The principle that physical identity also implies mental identity tells us nothing new about the world, since two physically identical events are, by definition, one and the same event. Neither does the thesis of global supervenience as such entail any theory about how physical and mental events are interdependent, unless one adds another metaphysical assumption, namely that all mental events are to be explained in a bottom-up way on the basis of the explanatory schemes of fundamental

---

[11] In 'The Individuation of Events' from 1969, Davidson defines uniqueness causally: 'events are identical if and only if they have exactly the same causes and effects' (1980, 179). Later, in 1985, he abandons this view in favor of Quine's position that 'Events are identical if and only if they occur in the same space at the same time' (cited by Evnine 1991, 28). Observe that on both accounts, sameness of physical features, including relations to all other events, implies strict identity!

physics. After all, global physicalist supervenience involves an empty circularity.

It seems that there is only one way out of this vacuity for the physicalist supervenience theorist. He or she must add to supervenience the grand-scale metaphysical claim that the whole history of human culture (including particulars such as Brutus stabbing Caesar and my writing this article) could be fully explained by the laws of fundamental physics. I would grant that this resort to a hidden but universal deterministic explanation of human cultures remains a metaphysical possibility. But it is also clear that it is utterly implausible both in face of what we know, and in face of what we don't know about our universe. *Physicalist supervenience is vacuous unless it adds a metaphysical hypothesis of complete determination which is scientifically unaccountable and extremely counter-intuitive.*[12]

A Model for Holist Supervenience

The example of St Francis draws our attention to the pivotal fact that higher-order consciousness inescapably depends on extrinsic cultural and social features that are not mirrored in the physical structure of an individual brain. Certainly, brains have a localized structure where different functions are exercised in different parts of the brain. Nonetheless the major part of our mental life is characterized by holistic features. The contents of our beliefs, the ideals guiding our choices, the aims of our desires, etc. are never determined by the character of individuals (and their brains), but depend on sociocultural facts of the linguistic communities to which we belong.

'Meanings ain't in our heads,' as it has been helpfully phrased by Hilary Putnam. The fact of mental holism implies that both reference and meaning depend upon society. It seems that the holism of the cultural realm shaping our subjective lives renders impossible the idea of a general causal reduction of mental states

---

[12] In the terms of Karl Popper (1992, 11–40), metaphysical determinism is a matter of belief, whereas the idea of a scientific determinism is a chimera, since one cannot account for the latter on the grounds of science.

to brain states (Putnam 1995, 443–5, cf. 406–15).[13] All of our higher-order experiences are codetermined by a social reality in which intentional objects are connected with one another in vast networks of meanings. If this is so, the so-called brain–mind problem should be seen in the context of the far more encompassing issue of the *brain–culture problem*.[14]

For this purpose Karl Popper has introduced a helpful distinction between a World 1 of physical facts, a World 2 of mental states, and a World 3 consisting of the constructs of human culture.[15] Popper rightly points out that we cannot discuss the mind–body problem appropriately unless we draw the institutional facts of World 3 into account (Popper 1994, 7f.). During a discussion, for example, I 'understand' (World 2) what my dialogue partner says, and I hope to 'follow his or her argument' (World 3). Through World 3, the fluctuating world of consciousness (World 2) is both shaped and pruned.

Notice that the physiological brain states (World 1) are usually irrelevant for determining the exact content of meanings. Meanings are not placed inside our skulls but make up a relational pattern which includes the social, psychological and natural environment of a language user. Microphysical brain states cannot make a pledge, a mouth cannot promise anything, only *persons* can do so – and even they can do so only inside given social settings. There is no 'deeper level' for a pledge or a promise to be sought. As recently emphasized by philosopher Lynne Rudder Baker in her argument

---

[13] Please observe that I am not saying here that brains do not produce consciousness, but I am saying that the local brain's production of consciousness cannot in itself explain the variety of particular experiential contents of this or that person – contents that often (in the case of 'higher consciousness') have global properties such as ideas of gravity, of human rights, of God, etc.

[14] Both Davidson's clarification of his earlier theory and Putnam's retraction of his earlier functionalism are dependent upon the insight of the 'holism' of the linguistic systems (an insight going back to W. V. O. Quine). Evnine (1991, 71) notices that Davidson's growing understanding of the externality of experiential contents implies that 'he no longer holds to supervenience in the way he originally conceived of it.'

[15] The three-world theory is developed in a rich and accessible form in Karl R. Popper (1994). Though Popper himself is a mind–body dualist, my appropriation of the three-world distinction is independent of his dualism.

for a 'practical realism,' one's mental states of believing and behaving depend on 'global properties,' including relations and
ultimate assumptions about what is possible and what is not
possible (1995, 22).

Such background assumptions and, ultimately, faith horizons
about factuals and counterfactuals make the mental into a holist
realm, a realm no longer treatable in terms of the outflows of
solitary brains. 'My pencil is cleverer than I am,' as Einstein said
with reference to the mathematical structures of World 3. However,
not only mathematics, geometry, logic, but also legal systems,
ethical codes, notions of self and of God contain such features of
universal width. Even our everyday coping with reality includes a
tacit reference to global properties which are present to us, sometimes clearly, sometimes dimly.

Moreover, by orientating ourselves in the social and cultural
world, we are presupposing that some elements of our culturally
constructed world (World 3) are in touch with objective relationships that presumably have a basis in reality apart from our perception of them. For instance, by following an argument, by
searching for truth, by coping with theoretical problems, by attun-
ing oneself to a harmony of truth and goodness, by believing in
God through the filters of human languages, we presuppose that
certain aspects of World 3 have some autonomy of its own vis-à-
vis our ephemeral World-2 states. We presuppose that some World-
3 moral codes consist not only of personal preferences, but also of
trans-subjective values. Likewise, we presuppose that some
elements of our sciences are not only constructions, but constitute
discoveries of some facets of 'reality.' Needless to say, both science
and religion are cultural activities which rely on this presupposition.

What are the metaphysical implications of ascribing a causal role
to the mental according to the basic assumptions of the holistic
supervenience theory? Figure 2 attempts to visualize some
important aspects. It appears from this figure that holist supervenience assumes a *constitutional physicalism*. That is, one does not
need to introduce separate 'psychic' or 'spiritual' elements in order
to understand the mental and the cultural realms. This would only

lead us back to a substance metaphysics. But exactly *relationality* is the key feature of the holist supervenience model, since the copresence of the network of World-3 contents in the subjective apprehension of World 2 is the key to understanding the onto-logical and causal roles of the supervenient properties.

FIGURE 2: A MODEL OF A HOLISTIC SUPERVENIENCE THEORY

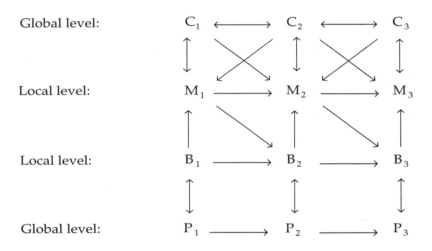

Global level:

Local level:

Local level:

Global level:

P denotes the global physical situation; B the local brain state; M the subjective mental state; C the holist relam of cultural contents. Observe that there is a one-directional arrow of time leading from $P_1 \to P_3$ and from $B_1 \to B_3$, whereas C makes up a realm of logically or semantically interconnected symbolic contents ($C_1 \leftrightarrow C_3$). Note also that the influence of B_1 on M_1 is temporally prior to the emerging feedback processes of M_1 on B_2. The causal impact of consciousness ($M_1 \to B_2$), is provided by the structuring capacity of experiential awareness. In the case of higher-order consciousness the relative autonomy of the mental is supported by the holistic realm of C which is copresent to M_2 as memory (C_1), as presentational immediacy (C_2), and as anticipation of future possibilities (C_3).

Consciousness may be described as a brain-based emergent property of natural evolution. However, it is an unusual property, for neither primary consciousness nor second-order consciousness can be described in purely physical terms. We therefore have to acknowledge the *semantic non-reductionism* of mental properties (non-reductionism1). But more than that, I have also argued that higher-order consciousness exercises a kind of *process autonomy*, that is, consciousness, by participating in a holistic mental realm, also plays a causal role (non-reductionism2). An awareness of this particular *quale* (e.g. the color red) leads on to an awareness of other *qualia* (the color blue) within the wider texture of World-2 colors. In the case of symbolic contents, the fact of process autonomy comes even more to the fore. Through languages and images, human persons acquire an openness of mind both for past and future, and a sense for enduring relationships and objects, such as scientific laws and entities, conceptions of goodness and beauty, and of God. As awareness leads to awareness (World 2), symbolic contents refer to other symbolic contents (World 3), and make up a holist texture which influences the behavior of individuals.

Supervenience and Special Divine Action: The Eucharist Model

Against the background of holist supervenience theory it is interesting that traditional sacramental theology consistently correlates God's transformation of the individual human mind or 'heart' with a coordination of material elements and symbolic contents. In the following interpretation of the active presence of Christ in the Eucharist, I aim to show that Luther, in particular, underlines that the believer's 'spiritual' transformation (World 2) is always brought about through a resonance between the physical signs (World 1) and God's symbolically encoded promises (World 3). A sacramental theology may thus present a model for conceptualizing God's special action in the framework of holist supervenience. According to Luther, God influences human minds 'in, with and under' the interplay between type-different (yet interacting) causalities.

World 1, World 2, World 3 in Baptism: From Augustine to Popper
According to basic Christian assumptions, God's works of creation begin and end in corporeality. From the purview of sacramental

theology, Christian existence also takes its point of departure from a certain bodily event, namely *baptism*. It is hardly a coincidence that in this prime example of a 'special divine action' the physical, the sociocultural and the psychological realms are attuned to one another.

First, we have the tangible, visible and audible *signs:* clean water, the pouring of water over the head or body, the signing of the cross, the phonetic aspects of speech, the gestures of the participants – all this belongs to the physico-biological realm of World 1. Unnegotiably, baptism 'takes place' at a given location and at a given time. Second, we have the specific theological *contents* involved in the different speech acts: the doxology, the readings from scripture, the blessing in connection with the sign of the cross, the confession, the prayer, the instruction – all this relates to World 3, the realm of symbolic meanings centered around the divine promise as instituted by Christ (Matt 28:18–20). Even if the event of baptism in World 1 is a short-term event, the divine promise (which makes the social event of baptism into a recognizable divine action) implies an endurance for this life and for the coming life of resurrection. Third, baptism cannot be performed without a baptismal candidate who is receiving the divine promise in *faith;* the confession of 'I believe ...' anticipates the child's future life-story as a continuous return to the divine promise in the extrinsic existence of faith. As such, faith definitely belongs to World 2, comprising both conscious and subconscious levels of mind. However, the claim that baptism is God's work is not given with the causal role of faith as such, but faith is claimed to make a difference with reference to the baptized person's *relatedness* to the publicly uttered (but individually addressed) divine promise. The World-2 states of faith are thus nourished by the World-3 contents of the communally expressed faith.

In this respect, Karl Popper's distinction between World 1, World 2 and World 3 reminds us of the classical Augustinian distinction between the *signum* of the sacraments (the spatio-temporally located signs), the *res* of the sacraments (the symbolic meanings of signs and words), and, above all, the *utilitas* of the sacraments (namely, the *use* of the signs in the mode of faith). Augustine developed this distinction under the assumption that whereas the signs are 'outer' and corporeal, symbolic meanings are 'inner' and spiritual. And since only 'the spirit within' comprehends the spiritual (cf. 1 Cor 2:10–13), Augustine conceptualized faith as an 'inner organ' which is actualized when the Holy Spirit illuminates the human soul and mind, so that it can capture and adhere to the 'inner Word' of God, Christ.

I am convinced, however, that it is possible to give a fully satisfactory theological account of God's special activity without this Augustinian presupposition of two parallel worlds. An aid that helps us move in this direction is Martin Luther's emphasis upon faith as grounded on the external word (*verbum externum*). In Luther's early eucharistic theology we find a consistent interrelation of physical, personal and social realms in his account of the active presence of Jesus Christ in the eucharistic meal.[16] Thus a 'thick' account of divine action with human minds, developed on the basis of a Christian self-description, is possible on a non-dualistic basis – provided, as we shall see, that the peculiarities of the mental realm of Worlds 2 and 3 are safeguarded.

World 1, World 2 and World 3 in Luther's Eucharistic Theology

Compared with baptism, the Eucharist is a repeatable event which has habitual character and is learned through a long-term practice of participation. Being a pivotal locus of Christian identity, the Eucharist is 'a corporate practice rather than, say, an ethical code, a world-view, a set of doctrines, an institutional constitution, a book, or some other distinctive feature' (Ford 1999, 140). As such, the Eucharist makes up a prime example of a life-historical interpenetration between an individual believer and his or her community.

Accordingly, on Luther's understanding, the social event of the Eucharist is more than a brief occasion in physical space; it is an

---

[16] In the following I draw upon my analysis (1996) of Luther's eucharistic theology, esp. as developed in the early treatise on *The Blessed Sacrament of the Holy and True Body of Christ* (Luther [1519] 1960), without in the present context going into textual details.

interaction between communicants as well as an interaction between God and believers. The presence of Christ is not claimed as the 'coming' of an absent Lord but rather as the 'emergence' or manifestation of Christ who is already omnipresent in the world of creation.

The claim of the effective presence of Christ in the Eucharist thus presupposes a variety of ontological commitments. It is presupposed that Christ is one with God the Father and shares with the Father and the Spirit an ubiquity in creation both as giver and as sustainer of life. There is a oneness between Christ and the Father. But the Eucharist also presupposes a unity between Christ and the believers. Christ is seen as the head of the 'body of Christ' (that is, the community of believers) in which Christ is present in a self-revelatory way. God may be omnipresent, but God is only manifest in happenings that are conformal with the love that God *is*. Luther can even say that the 'meaning and effect' (*Bedeutung und Werck*) of the Eucharist *is* the fellowship of believers, whence it derives its name as *communio* (Luther 1960, 50f.). Participating in the Eucharist means being ever deeper incorporated into this body of love.

The communion of faith is called 'spiritual' by Luther since it is comprised of all believers throughout all times and is constituted by Christ, its head. So far, the meaning of the Eucharist might appear somewhat vague. Indeed the 'meaning' of the Eucharist is not identical with occurrences that can be described in a physicalist language, nor for that reason in a purely psychological or sociological language. After all, the eucharistic participants are immersed in a larger story of faith and love that transcends the local congregation. Moreover, the meal and the gathering (World 1) and the believer's remembrance and reception of words and elements in faith (Worlds 2 and 3) are also, 'where and when it pleases God,' a coming forth of the particular presence of Jesus Christ. Christ is the *agent of incorporation*,[17] who is

---

[17] The importance of the motive of incorporation is rightly highlighted in David Ford's interpretation of the 'Eucharistic self' (Ford 1999, 137–65).

active in and through physical signs, words of culture, and mental apprehensions.

Accordingly, there is no faith in the believer apart from the faith evoked by the *external* word of promise and exhortation: 'This bread is my body that is for you. Do this in remembrance of me' (1 Cor 11:24). Neither is there any love in the believer apart from the love expressed in relation to the concrete congregation, the concrete neighbor. A transformation has always to occur in the believer:

> For the natural without the spiritual profits us nothing in this sacrament: a change [*Vorwandlung*] must occur [in the communicant] and be exercised through love. (Luther 1960, 62)

A divine action no less radical than the one claimed in the Roman Catholic doctrine of transubstantiation is here articulated as taking place *in the mind of the believer* (as we would say today). Just as many particles become one bread and drink, so too are the participants 'to be changed into one another through love' (1960, 62).

In this way, the very 'meaning' of the sacrament only comes to the fore in and through the right 'use' (intent, attitude, practice) of the elements and words of the Eucharist by the believers. In Luther's reappropriation of Augustine's threefold scheme, the 'meaning' (*res*) and the 'effect' (*utilitas*) coincide. Or, in Popper's terminology, the individual believer (World 2) is only changed by virtue of the exterior natural elements (World 1) which open up a new spiritual horizon of hope (World 3). This spiritual horizon, however, is not free-floating but finds a concrete embodiment in the exteriority of the concrete congregation. *God's power to change minds is apparently not taking place in a disembodied setting, from soul to soul, but in a specific bio-cultural embodiment.* The subjective self (World 2) resonates with the exteriority of the pre-human signs of food and drink (World 1), interpreted as a divine promise, a testimony 'for you' (World 3). The particular resonance between *these* partakers of this *specific* meal in accordance with the inviting words of Christ *is* the turning point of grace. Correspondingly, the human exercise of love pouring out of this resonance *is* the transformative power of God. God the Giver is present in God's gifts (Peura 1997).

The 'Tensed' Self in the Light of God's Face

In addition to Luther's strong emphasis on the social, almost spatial, character of the Eucharist, one could also highlight the temporal aspects of the presence of Christ. The meaning and effects of the eucharistic meal are thus consistently related to a temporalized or 'tensed' self which remembers the past and anticipates a new future. The Eucharist recalls the past of Jesus' table fellowship with tax collectors and sinners and continues this fellowship with deserters (Peter) and betrayers (Judas). (Remember that Peter and Judas were present at the last supper on Maundy Thursday.) But the participants are also stretching out towards the future messianic banquet in the Kingdom of God. 'I tell you, I will never again drink of this fruit of the vine until that day when I drink it new with you in my Father's kingdom' (Matt 26:29).

The individual's life-story is thus shaped by a wider narrative: the community is the group that experiences God's story with humankind. This transcommunal aspect comes to the fore in Jesus' reference to the 'new covenant in his blood' (1 Cor 11:25), which alludes to the previous stories of divine covenants (with Noah, with Abraham, with Moses, with David), which are all taken up and renewed by Jesus.[18] Likewise the memory of the past is retained in the reference to the 'forgiveness of sins.' Forgiveness here does not mean a licence to forget the past, but a recovery of the past in the mode of hope. Remission of sins thus includes a confrontation with the past in the present without making a specific mode of confrontation (a certain degree of repentance, for instance) a

---

[18] It is important to this interpretation that the term 'new covenant' does not mean an abolishment of the old, but a reshaping of the divine promises offered in the Old Testament covenants. God's transformative actions never start from point zero, in an act of a *creatio nova ex nihilo*, but always in continuation of the past engraved in the brains and mental capacities of believers. Likewise, baptism is a 'new birth' (1 Pet 1:3) that takes up and remolds the human being who was already previously created in the image of God, that is, created for communication with God. Baptism is *not* a new creation departing from the old; the eucharistic meal is *not* a break with God's previous history with humankind.

precondition.[19] Thus, in the eucharistic meal, the remembrance of the past and the embrace of a new covenant corresponds to the recalling of sin and the recovery of hope. Indeed, in the human hope *is* the Holy Spirit. The logic of Luther's sacramental realism demands that the divine Giver is present in God's gifts.

Likewise, the repeated advent of Jesus Christ in the eucharistic meal takes up the promise of companionship expressed in the institutional words of baptism: 'and see, I am with you always' (Matt 28:18). A resonance is created between God's 'seeing' of the world, and the human beings' new mode of seeing and approaching the world. In the story from Creation to the Fall, God's original 'seeing' in enjoyment (Gen 1:31) had to give way to God's 'seeing' in judgement (cf. Isa 55). Now, after Christ, God's seeing is transformed into an accompanying 'seeing for' (in the baptism) and a 'seeing in acceptance' (in the Eucharist). This complex divine 'seeing' entails both a judgment of the past and its redemptive recovery.

In the divine promise, God invites any follower to actualize a new way of 'seeing' and 'taking' the world which resonates with the divine way of 'seeing' and 'taking' the world. A differentiation between present self and past self begins, and the future is opened for a 'new self' which 'takes' the future as an open space of divine disclosures, rather than as an array of specific expectations that the self has to 'measure up to.'[20] According to Luther, such change in the mind and activity of the believer could not be accomplished without the interpenetration of the World 1, World 2 and World 3 in the individual believer. For on a deep level, inaccessible to human minds, the three worlds are not ontologically separated,

---

[19] Recently Gregory L. Jones (1995, 105–13) has reminded of the fact that Jesus did not make the declaration of the remission of sins dependent upon repentance. However, remission of sin is not possible without a recalling of the past sin(s) (1995, 145 f.; 175–82).

[20] The theology of Rudolf Bultmann can be interpreted as an interpretation of the New Testament's proclamation of the necessary reshaping of the 'tensed self.' Recently Charley D. Hardwick has convincingly argued that Bultmann's existentialism is consistent with an empiricist, non-reductionist physicalism (1996, 158–206).

but interconnected aspects of the one and same reality of God's creation in which God is present.[21]

In conclusion, I have tried to demonstrate how the incarnational substructure of Christian theology is consonant with the presuppositions of a mind–body monism. In accordance with the expectations of holist supervenience theory, the efficacy of God's transformation of human minds requires a simultaneous incarnation of God in World 1, in World 2, and in World 3.[22] From the purview of a Christian sacramental realism, God's particular influence on human minds takes place in the cross-fertilization between states of bodily conditions, states of consciousness, and the holist realm of the mental. The role traditionally appropriated to the Holy Spirit takes the form of a qualitative proliferation of this interplay. 'Special divine actions' take place in the public world as a personal address rather than as a hidden influence behind the backs of human beings.

References

ALEXANDER, SAMUEL. 1920. *Space, Time, and Deity: The Gifford Lectures at Glasgow 1916–18*, 2 vols, New York: The Humanities Press.

BAKER, LYNNE RUDDER. 1995. *Explaining Attitudes: A Practical Approach to the Mind*, New York: Cambridge University Press.

BIELFELDT, DENNIS. 1995. 'God, Physicalism, and Supervenience,' *CTNS Bulletin* 15.1, 1–12.

——. 1999. 'Supervenience as a Strategy of Relating Physical and Theological Properties,' *Studies in Science and Theology*, vol. 5, 163–76.

BIELFELDT, DENNIS. 2000. 'The Peril and Promise of Supervenience for the Science–Theology Discussion' (in this volume).

---

[21] In a Christian perspective, the unity of the world is constituted by God, and not by some immanent substrate of the world. In this sense, Christian faith can embrace monism, but not physicalism, at least not without some interpretative qualifications.

[22] Against Apollinarianism orthodox Christology rightly taught that Christ not only assumed 'flesh' in general (World 1) , but inhabited a particular human mind (World 2) – even a particular human culture (World 3), I would add.

BROWN, WARREN S., NANCEY MURPHY, H. NEWTON MALONY (eds). 1998. *Whatever Happened to the Soul? Scientific and Theological Portraits of Human Nature*, Minneapolis: Fortress Press.

CLAYTON, PHILIP. 1997. *God and Contemporary Science*, Grand Rapids: Eerdmans.

DAVIDSON, DONALD. 1980. *Essays on Actions and Events*, Oxford: Clarendon Press.

——. 1984. *Inquiries into Truth and Interpretation*, Oxford: Clarendon Press.

——. [1993] 1995. 'Thinking Causes,' in J. Heil, and A. Mele (eds), *Mental Causation*, Oxford: Clarendon Press, 3–18.

EDELMAN, GERALD M. 1992. *Bright Air, Brilliant Fire: On the Matter of the Mind*, New York: BasicBooks.

EVNINE, SIMON. 1991. *Donald Davidson*, Stanford: Stanford University Press.

FODOR, JERRY and ERNEST LEPORE. [1992] 1993. *Holism: A Shopper's Guide*, Oxford: Blackwell.

FORD, DAVID. 1999. *Self and Salvation: Being Transformed*, Cambridge: Cambridge University Press.

GREGERSEN, NIELS HENRIK. 1996. 'The Chalcedonian Structure of Martin Luther's Sacramental Realism,' in D. Lange and P. Widmann (eds), *Kirche zwischen Heilsbotschaft und Lebenswirklichkeit* (Festschrift Theodor Jørgensen), Frankfurt a.M.: Peter Lang, 177–96.

——. 1998a. 'A Contextual Coherence Theory for the Science–Theology Dialogue,' in N. H. Gregersen and J. W. van Huyssteen (eds), *Rethinking Theology and Science: Six Models for the Current Dialogue*, Grand Rapids: Eerdmans, 181–231.

——. 1998b. 'The Idea of Creation and the Theory of Autopoietic Processes,' *Zygon* 33, 333–67.

HARDWICK, CHARLEY D. 1996. *Events of Grace: Naturalism, Existentialism, and Theology*, Cambridge: Cambridge University Press.

HARE, R. M. [1988] 1990. 'Comments,' in D. Seanor and N. Fotion (eds), *Hare and Critics: Essays on 'Moral Thinking,'* Oxford: Clarendon Press.

JONES, GREGORY L. 1995. *Embodying Forgiveness: A Theological Analysis,* Grand Rapids: Eerdmans Publishing House.

KIM, JAEGWON. [1993] 1995a. *Supervenience and Mind: Selected Philosophical Essays,* Cambridge: Cambridge University Press.

———. [1993] 1995b. 'Can Supervenience Save Anomalous Monism?,' in J. Heil and A. Mele (eds.), *Mental Causation,* Oxford: Clarendon Press, 19–26.

LUTHER, MARTIN. [1519] 1960. 'The Blessed Sacrament of the Holy and True Body of Christ, and the Brotherhoods,' in *Luther's Works,* vol. 35, Philadelphia: Fortress Press, 45–74.

McLAUGHLIN, BRIAN P. 1995. 'Philosophy of Mind,' in R. Audi (ed.), *The Cambridge Dictionary of Philosophy,* Cambridge: Cambridge University Press, 597–606.

MURPHY, NANCEY. 1997. *Anglo-American Postmodernity: Philosophical Perspectives on Science, Religion, and Ethics,* Boulder: Westview Press.

———. 1998. 'Nonreductive Physicalism: Philosophical Issues,' in W. S. Brown, N. Murphy and H. N. Malony (eds), *Whatever Happened to the Soul? Scientific and Theological Portraits of Human Nature,* Minneapolis: Fortress Press, 127–48.

—— and GEORGE F. R. ELLIS. 1996. *On the Moral Nature of the Universe: Theology, Cosmology, and Ethics,* Minneapolis: Fortress Press.

NYBORG, HELMUTH. 1997. 'Molecular Man in a Molecular World: Applied Physiology,' *Psyke and Logos* 18, 457–74.

O'CONNOR, TIMOTHY. 1994. 'Emergent Properties,' *American Philosophical Quarterly* 31, 91–104.

PEACOCKE, ARTHUR. [1990] 1993. *Theology for a Scientific Age: Being and Becoming – Natural, Divine and Human,* London: SCM Press.

PEURA, SIMO. 1997. 'Christus als Gunst und Gabe,' in O. Bayer, R. W. Jenson and S. Knuuttila (eds), *Caritas Dei: Beiträge zum Verständnis Luthers und der gegenwärtigen Ökumene*, Helsinki: Luther-Agricola-Gesellschaft, 340–63.

POPPER, KARL R. [1982] 1992. *The Open Universe: An Argument for Indeterminism*, London and New York: Routledge.

———. 1994. *Knowledge and the Body–Mind Problem: In Defense of Interaction*, London and New York: Routledge.

PUTNAM, HILARY. [1994] 1995. *Words and Life*, Cambridge, Mass.: Harvard University Press.

SEARLE, JOHN R. 1995. *The Construction of Social Reality*, New York: The Free Press.

TESKE, JOHN A. 2000. 'The Social Construction of the Human Spirit' (in this volume).

9

The Social Construction of the Human Spirit

JOHN A. TESKE

As an academic psychologist I think it is important to see what our understanding of spirituality might inherit from our understanding of our psychology. From the viewpoint of psychology, one can no more see spirit as separate from nature than one can see mind as anything but deeply dependent upon the evolution of nervous systems of a particular form and complexity. Even if not sufficient to it, mental life, the life of emotion, cognition, and consciousness of self, is necessary for spirituality. Moreover, mental life itself only emerges through a long period of individual development, requiring lengthy dependency on other human beings, and extensive social support. This dependency and support not only meets, but shapes our biological and emotional needs, and brings our cognitive capacities and our personhood into being, building within each of us an identity and an interior life. Given the role of interdependence in the emergence of individual minds, any integrity we have as spiritual beings is likely also to be an achievement contingent upon the character of our relationships with other persons, and our memberships in larger communities. If so, understanding our spirituality requires sustained attention to its social nature. If our emotional lives, our inner subjectivity, and the boundaries of our individual identities are historically developed constructions (even if equipped and required by our biological inheritance), then it is possible, as a social and spiritual project, to reconstruct and transform our lives in alternative ways, recognizing the interdependencies that are our real source of strength and power, and becoming more attentive to our moral fellowship with others.

In recent articles, I argued that neuropsychology is necessary but insufficient to account for the human spirit (Teske 1996), and that its emergence is evolutionarily and developmentally rooted in social interdependence (Teske 1998). The present paper specifically addresses the processes which may be involved in the social construction of the human spirit. The human spirit is taken to be that aspect of human mental life by which we can apprehend meanings and purposes extending beyond our individual lives. It is possible that the transcendence of the spirit over individual neurocognition is neither a fiction, nor an illusion, but a product of social life which cannot be accounted for in terms of individual psychology alone. The specific thesis of the present paper is that the human spirit can be understood as a social and historical construction, dependent upon but not determined by human neuropsychology, in turn embedded within the evolutionary emergence of higher mental processes.

The Evolution of Neuropsychological Constituents: Review of Previous Argument

The present argument will presuppose (1) that individual neuro-psychology is necessary but insufficient to account for the integrity of self and spirit, and (2) that this is a fragile achievement which is contingent, for both evolutionary and ontogenetic reasons, on the construction of the person, of emotional life, of internal subjective experience, and of the boundaries of individuality. In a recent article (Teske 1996) I argued that spirituality, defined as the apprehension of meanings and purposes extending beyond the individual, required a neuropsychology sufficient to represent both self and world. While accounting for some of the requisites of spiritual life, like sentience, conscious mental life, and self-knowledge, our neuropsychology also helps us understand their limitations. The 'modularity' of our neuropsychology in particular (the tendency of our brains to function as a set of semi-autonomous subsystems), while necessary for the stabilization of a complex neural system, raises a 'problem of integrity,' evidenced by research on hemispheric differences, brain dysfunction, and even the dissociations present in normal memory. What I suggest is that the integrity of self or spirit needs to be understood as an achievement and, while systems of belief, as well as subdoxastic emotional integrations, may contribute to this achievement, it is largely produced via our position within larger systems or communities. Spiritual integrity therefore depends upon the psychological interiorization of purposes which themselves transcend individual mentality. Surrender and sacrifice can then be understood to require a desacralization of boundaries of self. That is, that we no longer take the boundaries of self as given or obvious, as natural kinds or as ordained by God, but in fact as sociohistorically constructed human products, however sedimented and buried in time they may be, and appreciate that we are also capable of more deeply understanding or even transforming them, both within and beyond our own lives.

I recently argued in these pages (Teske 1998) that the human neuropsychology necessary for spirituality has an evolutionary history requiring extensive social interdependency for its development. The immaturity of human nervous systems at birth, and their plasticity, results in a need for experiential shaping, which continues through the course of an individual's life. The evolutionary hypertrophy of the prefrontal cortex in particular (i.e. its growth well beyond the previous hominid proportions), which colonizes the neural regulation of arousal, and affects the very structure of emotional life, results in a need for extensive social scaffolding for normal human functioning (the size and location of the enlarged parts of the brain results in their appropriation or influence upon a wide range of other functions). This makes possible the emergence of a socially constructed virtual reality (the use of a metaphor of 'virtual reality' should, I hope, be evocative for anyone who has ever fully engaged in an interactive computer game), a supervenient symbolic world transcending immediate experience. Our engagement with such a world is rooted in familial and communal attachments which generate the emotional and spiritual patterns of adulthood. Our cognitive capacities involve a symbolic independence from immediate environments, and make possible the emergence of symbioses with external memory systems. Such systems make possible novel and interiorized forms of socially constituted experience, including the spiritual.

Processes of Social Construction Relevant to Spirituality

Given the deep evolutionary and ontogenetic role of social inter-dependence in human mental life, the integrity of self and spirit is an achievement likely to be contingent upon our membership in relational and communal wholes of which our minds, selves, and spirits are but parts, and upon which their larger meanings depend. The specific character of human emotional life, our inner subjectivities, and even the boundaries of our individuality are socially constructed and maintained. It is likely that even 'internal states' are constituted within a semantic rather than a physical space, itself a social and intellectual product.

The argument for the social construction of the human spirit builds on the 'constitutive rules' of John Searle, and will suggest how the specific character of human emotional life (as understood by psychologists, psychoanalysts, and anthropologists), our inner subjectivities (understood via classic and contemporary work on the social origins of individual cognition), the boundaries of our individuality (as understood psychologically, anthropologically, and even historically), may be socially constructed and maintained. Evidence for the social construction of biologically rooted emotional life, both across development and across cultures, will be presented, suggesting an analogous construction of spiritual sentiments. I will argue (drawing on work in both psychology and philosophy) that even 'internal states' are constituted within a semantic rather than a physical space, itself a social and intellectual product which, while dependent on individual neuropsychology, is not necessarily coterminous with it. Indeed, the boundaries between this semantic space and the world 'outside' is the central issue in therapeutic discourse. Argument will be made for the social construction and cultural limitations of our particular form of individuality, to show how individuality might be capable of transformation, by considering alternative constructions. I will also look more deeply at the role of narrative, culturally and historically rooted, unified by tradition and community, as a *sine qua non* of both identity and a moral or spiritual life. Finally, I will conclude with a review of the theologically relevant elements of the present account of spirituality, and suggest some resources for explicating a theology more attentive to the social nature of our selves and spirits.

Constitutive Rules

Searle's (1969, 1995) concept of a 'constitutive rule' provides a paradigm case of how social construction works. Regulative rules, like the driving code, regulate antecedently existing activity (driving) which is logically independent of the rules. Constitutive rules, like the rules of American Football, create new forms of behavior (touchdown, offsides) whose existence is logically dependent on the rules. These rules constitute activities, events, or objects, called 'institutional facts' (*v.* 'brute facts') by Searle, which would not exist without the rules. Mating would exist without such rules, but not marriage, nor divorce. Physical possession of objects would exist, but what of ownership, property? Constitutive rules ramify even into our personal lives. Relationships like 'friend' vary across cultures, subcultures, and historical eras. There are things one 'cannot do' and still be a friend.

Institutional facts, like the existence of restaurants, waiters, or even dollars (Searle 1995), while they cannot exist without physical tokens (whether relatively localized, as in the case of a dollar, or distributed over space and time, as in the case of a marriage), cannot be defined in terms of any particular physico-chemical description. A dollar can be metal, paper, wampum, or even magnetic traces on a computer disk. Still, institutional facts, like the fact that the metal objects in my pocket are money, are only *epistemically* objective, in that they are true independently of any individual's representations; they are *ontologically* subjective in that they are facts only relative to the intentionality of agents. They are also language dependent, both epistemically, and because of their communicability, complexity, and independence of the attitudes of specific participants (e.g. I may still be married, even if I have forgotten that I am), ontologically. Money, like marriage, only *is* what it is because some particular human beings are prepared to treat its tokens in certain ways (although they can change historically). So, unlike brute facts, institutional facts do not exist independently of *all* representations, but are observer-relative functions rather than intrinsic properties, even if the observer-relativity is collective and social.

Institutional facts can be iterated. Having the functional and moral status of husband and wife requires the institutional fact of marriage, which requires a marriage ceremony, which requires a certain kind of social contract, which requires making a promise, which, in turn, requires a certain form of linguistic utterance. The logical structure of complex societies is provided by such iteration, interlocked into systems, maintained and varied through time, accumulated and sedimented historically. These iterated structures are what grant symbolic powers for the creation of meaning, deontic powers for the creation of rights and obligations, and make possible the logical structure of social power and even honor. The iteration and interlocking of institutional facts means that they cannot exist in isolation, that they are fundamentally systemic (Searle 1995). By virtue of their historical sedimentation, they may appear to be more obdurate facts, and it may require some effort to uncover their sources. Nevertheless, as Searle points out, what *enables* observers to create or impose such institutional functions *is* intrinsic to observers. Given the demonstrable developmental, cultural, and historical variation in the attribution of personhood, or in the life of the human spirit, it seems uncontroversial to assert their institutional character. Nevertheless, one can take issue with Searle *vis-à-vis* whether mental states are themselves intrinsic to observers, or observer-relative functions only made possible by neurological processes which are intrinsic to observers.

There are a number of events, conventionally viewed by psychologists to be, by virtue of their locatability within individual subjective experience, intrinsic or 'natural' properties of individuals. These include characteristics of both our cognitive and our emotional lives which research suggests may be locatable, as much in structure and operation as in content, socially rather than individually, *between* rather than *inside* persons. If central and essential components of our understanding and experience of the world are socially constructed, then it follows that the subset of our understanding and experience which constitutes our spirituality (including our ability to apprehend, emotionally engage with, internalize, identify with, and direct our lives toward meanings or purposes transcending the self), is likely to be similarly embedded. We turn now to three such components: emotional life, psychological internality, and individuality itself.

Emotional Life

The social construction of emotion is particularly relevant to spirituality. While emotions, like much of the rest of our embodied lives, may derive from evolutionarily constrained biological givens, they are understood, experienced, and enacted according to a particular set of historical and cultural rules. The basic structure of our emotional life is built in childhood out of foundational scenes which engage our biological systems. These foundational scenes are rooted in the character of family interactions scripted by the culture (Nathanson 1992, Tomkins 1979). Emotions are 'intentional' states, they have objects, they are 'about' something (Averill 1980). It is the experience of the relationship to this object that constitutes the meaning of the emotion, or, more accurately, is constituted by it, since it is the experience that is going to be generated by the supervenience of meaning upon biology, not vice versa. This is because it is the sharing in a common stock of knowledge about that kind of relation which enables a person to act in an intelligent and appropriate manner (Shotter 1984).

Averill defines emotion as 'a transitory social role (a socially constituted syndrome) that includes an individual's appraisal of the situation and that is interpreted as a passion rather than as an action' (1980, 312). Passivity is experienced as something that has *happened to me*, is beyond my control, rather than as something I have self-initiated, *done for myself*. The classification of any self-involving event as active or passive requires interpretation, an evaluation not inherent to the response itself, as in Schafer's (1976) psychoanalytic account of emotions as 'disclaimed actions.'

We see here how an important ego boundary, the intra-individual boundary between action and passion, is maintained. Nevertheless, such a definition of emotion makes clear that what is constituted by the social construction of our emotional lives is not just a set of internal states, but a complex set of relationships both with the objects of emotion, and with a cultural system which determines the overall drama. This overall drama includes not only our roles, but the parts played by others, including the generalized other, around which we build a more unified sense of self.

Such an account of emotion can easily be extended to the whole universe of 'spiritual' passions. If *all* emotions are so constructed, it makes no sense to suggest that *any* emotion is less real by virtue of such a process of construction, only that different social and historical contingencies may produce quite different but just as 'real' emotions. Consider an emotion of the Ilongot male, called *liget*, which irritates and distracts him until it reaches its peak, moving him to slice off the head of an enemy, thereby filling him with energy, passion and a deeper sense of knowledge (Rosaldo 1980). This is a cultural construction as much as our feelings of romantic love, or the passions of faith.

Psychological Internalization

The classic work on the social construction of thought is that of Vygotsky (1978) and Luria (1976), who present evidence about how inescapably social our 'inner' thoughts are. Vygotsky (1978) provides an example of a cognitive function that originates in a relation between mother and child in the way a child's reaching gets interpreted as pointing. It is in the child's relations with others that the meaning of situations is built, and only subsequently internalized, and Vygotsky's work suggests that this may be true for all the higher cognitive functions, including attention, memory, and the formation of concepts. Recent examples of the social construction of memory gone awry are provided by the problems associated with 'recovered' memories in the case of sexual abuse, e.g. Wright (1993). Luria's work (1976), particularly with Uzbekistan peasants, suggests that even the capacity for abstract reasoning is contingent on historical changes in social life and organization.

Rom Harre (1984) states as a principle that everything in the mind first existed in some conversation between experienced and novice members of the culture. The key to the process, which can be linked explicitly to the notion of a constitutive rule, is the 'psychological symbiosis' in which the mature person provides the immature with internal states by interacting with them *as though* they possessed them (Ochs and Schieffelin 1984). We 'internalize' these motives, intentions, and understandings by habituating the behavior scaffolded by others, acting *as if* we have those states, and, by the same process, being enjoined in the same constitutive discourse. If I successfully act 'as if' I were assertive, I am legitimately taken to be assertive. 'Internal states' are constituted within a semantic space which is itself a social product and which, while they certainly depend on the neurobiological operations by which each individual's piece of the process depends, are not necessarily coterminous with an individual's biological boundaries.

The origin of putatively individual cognitive activity in social context is amply documented in the psychological literature. Cognitive complexity, for example, is likely to be as much a property of social situation as of individuals. The research of Tetlock and Boettger (1989) suggests that social circumstances like crisis, personal threat, and even political campaigning are as likely to produce lower cognitive complexity as to be produced by it. Even the frequently replicated finding of an error in over-attributing internal causes of behavior (Nisbett and Borgida 1974; Ross, Amabile and Steinmetz 1977), may be attributed to internal processes by committing a meta-version of the same error (Jellison and Green 1981). Evidence both that this kind of error is made far less frequently in Mysore than in Chicago (Miller 1984), and that American subjects judged to be 'more socially adjusted' are more prone to this error (Block and Funder 1986), suggests that it is a cultural rule rather than a pan-human 'cognitive bias.'

Self-Contained Individualism

In the Western culture of which the Judeo-Christian tradition is a part, we take the existence of separate, autonomous individuals, with capacities for self-direction and responsibility to be self-evident (cf. Gergen 1991). We grant rights to individuals, we hold them responsible for their actions, and we hold single individuals to be the only appropriate containers of a whole range of emotions, from romantic love to the peace that passeth all understanding. To say that the particular form that our individuality takes is a social construction is, again, not to say that it is illusory, but that its reality is of an abstract, and socially negotiated kind, just as any other socially instituted entity.

The evidence from other cultures suggests that our conception of an individual self is constituted by a set of cultural roles and practices. This evidence suggests that the kind of bounded and autonomous individuality which we presume to be universal is instead culturally *peculiar* (Geertz 1973). As Heelas and Locke (1981) indicate, all cultures make some distinction between self and not-self, but differ radically both on their boundaries, and on the exist-ence of and the proper relations between various parts. For the Balinese there is only a minimal role for the unique, individual self in everyday life and it would border on the nonsensical to consider the state of individuals' minds in relating to them. For the Ilongot, there is no recognition of an autonomous self apart from outward behavior (Rosaldo 1984), and the collectivist Ifaluk find any reference to unique, autonomous individuality as excessively egocentric. Traditional Hindu culture defines the self fluidly in and through others rather than by sharp differentiation from them (Miller 1984; Shweder and Bourne 1982; Shweder and Miller 1985).

The Western conception of self is also historically recent. John Lyons (1978) argues that it was not until the late eighteenth century that people began to view their individual selves as central, previously viewing themselves in terms of group membership categories. Even the soul was not an individual possession, but created by God and made incarnate only transiently. In the medieval world, privacy did not mean separation from members of one's household but its separation from the wider public (Duby 1988). Roy Baumeister (1986, 1987) traces the contributing historical trends, including the religious choice introduced by the Reformation, the distinction between public and private self made possible by capitalism, and the cultivation of an inner self during the Romantic era. He sees identity as *the* spiritual problem of our time, as cultural change has produced a decline in the guidance produced by traditional religion, urbanization has increased the confusion of choice and distraction, life has been demystified by science, and psychology has undercut confidence in our self-knowledge. The contemporary Western 'self' is constituted by being socialized according to a particular theory (Harre 1985). We are taught to believe in a 'self' which has a rich interior, is clearly bounded from not-self, is construed to be the possession of a particular biological individual, and is assumed to be unique. It may be that the 'crisis and commitment' aspects thought to result in the achievement of identity (Erikson 1956, 1959, 1968) are themselves constructions produced by a certain sort of justificatory account rather than by intrapsychic processes. Following Winch (1958) and Wittgenstein (1953), Slugoski and Ginsburg (1989) argue that the requirements of identity achievement are isomorphic with the criteria for intelligibility of human action, that is, that being able to make one's actions intelligible is the same as having an identity. The criteria for intelligibility involve being able to give a reason for an action (whether or not the action was previously intended), and to be committed by that action to consistent future behavior. One claims an identity the same way one claims agency, by '[representing] one's actions as issuing from the workings of a complex cognitive machinery' (Harre 1979, 256). Not only is 'internality' itself a social construction, but it is the process of accounting for actions as intentional which maintains one's identity.

Alternative Individualisms

A case can be made that spiritual connections, connections via trans-individual meanings and purposes, between people and their intimates, their families, and their communities, have been socially *deconstructed*, rendered suspect, meaningless, or unintelligible. Historical and cultural forces have served to construct a self increasingly alienated from community, from tradition, and from shared meaning, as these social wholes are increasingly eroded and fragmented by the emergence of postmodern culture. What Sampson (1988) calls 'self-contained individualism' may be the historical product of the development of Western civilization, but it could hardly have produced such accomplishments as the building of cathedrals, the emergence of the scientific community, or the political unification of continents. The truly great achievements of any culture are not as likely to come from separate actors attempting to mesh, but from 'interdependent actors whose very design for being includes working on behalf of larger interests' (21). An alternative 'ensembled individualism' includes more fluid boundaries between self and other, locates control in a field of forces inclusive of the individual, and conceives of a self which includes relationships with others. Sampson presents evidence that the latter form of individualism is actually more common worldwide, providing illustrations from Maori, Hindu, Japanese, Confucian, and Islamic indigenous psychologies, as well as from Greek tragedy and pre-Homeric narrative. Sampson argues that defining internal control as freedom and external control as the lack thereof tends to conceal the overdetermining field of forces controlling any course of action, much of which is well outside of individual desire and will.

The point is that transcending the dominant view of self, and constructing spiritual connection, is not to be obtained by surrendering to the deconstructive forces of postmodernism (those forces which would erode or fragment meaning), but by recognizing, rather than denying, the hidden interdependencies that are the sources of strength and power for individuals. Ultimately it is only through this sort of reconstructive (in the sense of building greater and more coherent, more healing, structures of meaning) social project that spirit is constituted in any historical period – as it can be, anew, in ours.

Movement in Spiritual Space

Julian Jaynes (1976) and others (cf. Hermans, Kempen and van Loon 1992) argue that our very consciousness of self is constituted and organized metaphorically *as* a space. Moreover, if the social constitution of a kind of logical or moral space is a prerequisite of selfhood, the life of that self entails movement in that space, and it is in narrative that coherence and continuity, that particular connections between events, that the integration or the dis-integration of one's life through time, are constituted. Charles Taylor (1989) argues that it is only by virtue of having a location in a moral space that we can be said to have selves.

Taylor (1989) provides a detailed account of the historical emergence of our contemporary understanding of the self, in which he argues that, whether or not we are aware of it, some kind of moral framework is inescapable for selfhood. He argues that discussions of morality have focused too heavily on issues of respect and obligation for others, and not on two other axes, that of what makes for a full life and our dignity, or that which we believe commands the respect of others. If our very presence and movement in the world is shaped early on by an awareness of others, an awareness of a public space, then even if we come to question our moral framework, living in a space of communal and consequential values is constitutive of human agency. The moral space constitutes, and is incorporated into one's self-identity, such that one cannot step outside that space without damaging one's personhood. We can see this in the disorientation produced by identity crises, in the emptiness and vertigo of wider horizons being swept away in modern crises of meaninglessness, and even in pathological levels of ego loss which can affect one's grip on one's very stance in physical space. Taylor also makes clear that, unlike independent objects of scientific discourse, a self only exists among others, in 'webs of interlocution,' in a geography of social space, 'and also crucially in the space of moral and spiritual orientation within which my most important defining relations are lived out' (47).

Despite his attention to the public nature of the moral space within which our self-identity is constituted, much of Taylor's (1989) book is at pains to explore the emergence of our peculiarly modern notion of inwardness, a version of which we have already rehearsed here. In my view, what much of contemporary selfhood, and hence personhood, is about is a kind of incorporation or 'interiorization' of a moral space. With Taylor, I agree that understanding my location in moral space, what moves me, and what is the direction of my life requires narration. To build a life worth living is to build some greater reality or story into our lives. To the extent that this includes aspirations for transcending one's finite, human desires and beliefs, this is the story of our spirituality, whether theistically based or not. 'In order to have a sense of who we are, we have to have a notion of how we have *become*, and of where we are *going*' (47), so 'because we cannot but orient ourselves to the good, and this determines our place relative to it and hence determining the direction of our lives, we must inescapably understand our lives in narrative form, as a "quest"' (51). Taylor finds our placement and orientation within, and the narrative of our movement within a moral space to be 'inescapable structural requirements of human agency' (51).

There is no doubt but that the ability to construct a narrative of one's life is supported by brain structures, though not necessarily one's own, but that one's own psychological 'interior,' including the moral space constituting one's agency, is not necessarily isomorphic with one's biological interior. The sense of meaning in our lives may only be possible through a kind of 'narrative truth,' as indicated by Donald Spence (1982) and Donald Polkinghorne (1988). Moreover, the narratives themselves, or at least the traditions from which they are derived, are sociohistorical products by definition. It is these narrative traditions that thinkers like Taylor (1989) and Alasdair MacIntyre (1981) would have us become aware of in seeing how we construct integrated lives. Traditions like the biblical and republican strands pointed to by Robert Bellah and his colleagues (1985) as well as the romanticist and modern languages described by Gergen (1991), are certainly important parts of the heritage of self in complex Western society. The roots of our very spirituality are also sociohistorical products, and that spirituality itself is always rooted in a narrative tradition, realized by a process of historically sedimented metaphorization. One need only reflect for a moment on the metaphors of God as father, realms of kingdoms and lords, and spirit as breath, to realize how much of a tradition is constructed out of the available languages of time and history.

The goal here has not been to deconstruct the self, or by implication, the possibility of an individually centered spiritual integrity, but only to illustrate the contingency of selfhood, and to suggest that there is an open-endedness to that contingency which leaves room for us, as a human community, to reconstruct in ways that enable the living of more meaningful, more spiritually integrated lives. It points away from a view of persons as having essences, or of having 'souls' in any way that escapes the socio-historical and evolutionarily embodied contingencies by which they are constituted. Spirituality includes the other in our construals of ourselves, and it is the solidarity with them that alone allows the story, our story, to outlive our individual biologies. The goal is never merely to preserve, to entomb, to repeat endlessly, to be reborn unchanged, but for growth, for procreation, to create anew, to be transformed.

Theological Relevance

In the context of the current science–theology discussion, it may be valuable to review the theologically relevant elements of the present account of spirituality. The first is that on this account, our spirituality is deeply embodied. It is necessarily rooted in and dependent on (but not determined by or reducible to) our neuro-psychology, tied to a certain level of cortical complexity. Nevertheless this tie to neuropsychology makes integrity a contingent achievement, heavily dependent on individual development, in which social and intellectual processes engage and shape deeper biological mechanisms. It is also evolutionarily rooted in capacities for neuroregulatory and emotional function, shaped by a social interdependence which helps account for the sociocultural symbioses so important for communal life.

The second theologically relevant element of spirituality is that it is historically contingent. Historical and social processes generate and constitute much of what we think of as our spirituality. There is a role for the historical emergence of rule-structures which bring new entities and events into being, events which while they may be constructed, are not, on that account, necessarily fictional. These historical processes are themselves evolutionarily embedded, but provide an additional route to the renewal and transformation of human life.

A third theologically relevant element is the social inter-dependence of our spiritual lives, linked to basic emotional attach-ments and their development. Our very cognitive abilities are likely to be socially originated, the interiorization of which may constitute central features of our spiritual experience. Nevertheless, attention to the interdependent character of our interior lives may make alternatives possible to the individual separation and alienation so endemic to the contemporary world. Ultimately this attention may require fuller explication in a theology which explicitly makes reference to religious communities.

Although I am by no means a theologian by training, it may be useful to suggest some resources for the theological task. Unfortun-ately, most of the work within the science–theology tradition, and in theology more generally, seems to take the existence of the individual person for granted as a natural kind. This appears, for example, in the focus on a tension between the biological adapta-tion of individuals and of groups (cf. Hefner 1993), which tends not to include an understanding that individuality itself may be a product of group adaptation, and that the 'tension' may contribute to the historical flexibility of group adaptation.

From the Anglo-American science–theology tradition the work of Barbour and Hefner are important resources. Barbour's (1990) attention to reorientation and the healing of brokenness as central theological components is significant. Along with Peacocke's attention (1993) to the emergence of distinct actions at higher levels of biological complexity, Barbour's multi-leveled emergentist view also takes evolution seriously. Barbour also draws attention to our evolution as social beings, and the impossibility of language or symbolic thought without it, and the dependence of our very sense of self on our treatment by others. Barbour's biblical view of human nature, acknowledging the social nature of individuals in community, also recovers the meaning of 'covenant,' with a people, 'not a succession of individuals,' and including a participative responsibility for the world, and the possibility of cultural transformation. Like Tillich (1957), Barbour sees sin in the violation of relatedness and interdependence, in egocentricity and inordinate self-love. Nevertheless, I think this understanding also needs to be balanced with Reinhold Niebuhr's (1964) observation that Western culture is indebted to religion for 'the sense of individuality and the sense of a meaningful history.' In the wake of this century's totalitarian politics, and the continued horrors produced by racial and ethnic hatred, we best heed his warning that the denial of individual limits (in which I would include our very individuality) also ramifies into (or perhaps, is a reflection of) an even greater tendency of groups, over individuals, to absolutize and to be blind to the rationalization of their self-interest.

Philip Hefner's (1993) theological theory of created co-creators is another important resource. While an appreciation for Hefner's work may belie my Lutheran heritage, I am not sanguine about his dualism of biology and culture. Hefner perceives our personhood as the 'weaver' or the 'gatekeeper' (Hefner 1998, 539 and 543). However, both these metaphors imply a separation between biology and culture which requires some form of reconnection. Hefner sees the natural order as a 'fit vehicle for divine grace' (1993, 232), and the core of the *imago Dei* as a free creator of meanings, emerging from a long evolutionary process, including a symbiotic co-evolution of biology and culture. Nevertheless, despite his sensitivity to the constitutive over referential functions of religious language and ritual, he does not carry this into an understanding that the individual per se may be a linguistically and culturally constituted entity. While it is still possible, with Hefner, to view our evolutionary heritage as an obstacle to moral life (although it may not be in many cases, e.g. reciprocal or kin-based altruism, capacities for empathy, the emotional bases for attachment and love), it may be that population genetics, group selection, and cultural symbioses might help us see how individual morality, and individuality itself, as constituted by modernity, can be transformed. Group life might be enhanced by individuation as well as by sacrifice. I agree with Hefner, nevertheless, about the importance of sacrifice, of giving oneself, even in death (ultimately necessary for evolutionary change), to units beyond the self. If the meaning of something just *is* its function in a larger system, then self-transcendence is involved in the very apprehension of meaning, something which thinkers like Tillich and Rahner might readily affirm. As I argue elsewhere (Teske 1999), giving oneself to something greater, the only meaning one's life can finally have, may require an end, a bounding of self. Hefner is also very sensitive to the need to construct narratives and symbols, a capacity 'intrinsic to the evolutionary process at the level of homo sapiens', to justify, explain, and assess action. I would again want to argue that actions, and even agency itself, are not merely 'contextualized' or 'marked linguistically' by such constructions, but are constituted by them. Narration and symbolization is not created *de novo* by individuals, since individual identity is itself constituted, generated, and brought into being as a sociohistorical and developmental product via such narration and symbolization.

There are a whole range of ways in which the present account of spirituality may be theologically relevant in terms of meaning, morality, and even in our contemplation of mortality. It may be useful to understand the meaning of our lives in the movement in semantic and moral space that is narrative. We may better learn to understand how meaning and purpose can supervene on the development of more relational selves and spirits, especially as we understand just how transcendence is not bound to individual biology, and how self-transcendence requires not only separation from but openness to others, and to that which is Other.

References

AVERILL, JAMES R. 1980. 'A Constructivist View of Emotion,' in R. Pluchik and H. Kellerman (eds), *Emotion: Theory, Research, and Experience*, vol. 1: *Theories of Emotion*, Orlando, Fla.: Academic Press.

BARBOUR, IAN. 1990. *Religion in an Age of Science*, San Francisco: Harper & Row.

BAUMEISTER, ROY G. 1986. *Identity: Cultural Change and the Struggle for Self*, New York: Oxford University Press.

——. 1987. 'How the Self Became a Problem: A Psychological Review of Historical Research,' *Journal of Personality and Social Psychology* 52, 163–76.

BLOCK, JACK, and DAVID C. FUNDER. 1986. 'Social Roles and Social Perception: Individual Differences in Attribution and Error,' *Journal of Personality and Social Psychology* 51, 1200–7.

BELLAH, ROBERT N., RICHARD MADSEN, WILLIAM M. SULLIVAN, ANN SWIDLER and STEVEN TIPTON. 1985. *Habits of the Heart: Individualism and Commitment in American Life*, New York: Harper & Row.

DUBY, GEORGES. 1988. 'Solitude: Eleventh to Thirteenth Centuries,' in G. Duby (ed.), *A History of Private Life*, vol. 2: *Revelations of the Medieval World* 509-33, Cambridge, Mass.: Harvard University Press.

ERIKSON, ERIC H. 1956. 'The Problem of Ego Identity,' *Journal of the American Psychoanalytic Association* 4, 56–121.

——. 1959. *Identity and the Life Cycle*, New York: International Universities Press.

——. 1968. *Identity: Youth and Crisis*, New York: Norton.

GEERTZ, CLIFFORD. 1973. *The Interpretation of Cultures*, New York: BasicBooks.

GERGEN, KENNETH J. 1991. *The Saturated Self: Dilemmas of Identity in Contemporary Life*, New York: BasicBooks.

HARRÉ, ROM. 1979. *Social Being*, Oxford: Basil Blackwell.

HARRÉ, ROM. 1984. *Personal Being*, Cambridge, Mass.: Harvard University Press.

——. 1985. 'The Language Game of Self-Ascription: A Note,' in J. Shotter and K. J. Gergen (eds), *Texts of Identity*, Newbury Park, Calif.: Sage.

HEELAS, CARL, and ANDREW LOCKE (eds). 1981. *Indigenous Psychologies: The Anthropology of the Self*, New York: Academic Press.

HEFNER, PHILIP. 1993. *The Human Factor: Evolution, Culture, and Religion*, Minneapolis: Fortress Press.

——. 1998. 'The Spiritual Task of Religion in Culture: An Evolutionary Perspective,' *Zygon* 33, 535–44.

HERMANS, HUBERT J. M., HARRY J. G. KEMPEN and RENS J. P. VAN LOON. 1992. 'The Dialogical Self: Beyond Individualism and Rationalism,' *American Psychologist* 47, 23–33.

JAYNES, JULIAN. 1976. *The Origins of Consciousness in the Breakdown of the Bicameral Mind*, Boston: Houghton Mifflin.

JELLISON, JERALD M., and JANE GREEN. 1981. 'A Self-Presentational Approach to the Fundamental Attribution Error: The Norm of Internality,' *Journal of Personality and Social Psychology* 40, 643–9.

LURIA, ALEXANDER R. 1976. *Cognitive Development: Its Cultural and Social Foundations*, Cambridge, Mass.: Harvard University Press.

LYONS, JOHN O. 1978. *The Invention of the Self*, Carbondale, Ill.: Southern Illinois University Press.

MACINTYRE, ALASDAIR. 1981. *After Virtue*, Notre Dame, Ind: University of Notre Dame Press.

MILLER, JOAN. 1984. 'Culture and the Development of Everyday Social Explanation,' *Journal of Personality and Social Psychology* 46, 961–78.

NATHANSON, DONALD. 1992. *Shame and Pride: Affect, Sex, and the Birth of the Self*, New York: W. W. Norton.

NIEBUHR, REINHOLD. 1964. *The Nature and Destiny of Man*, New York: Scribner's.

NISBETT, RICHARD E., and EUGENE BORGIDA. 1975. 'Attribution and the Psychology of Prediction,' *Journal of Personality and Social Psychology* 32, 932–43.

OCHS, ELEANOR, and BAMBI B. SCHIEFFELIN. 1984. 'Language Acquisition and Socialization,' in R. A. Shweder and R. A. Levine (eds), *Culture Theory: Essays on Mind, Self, and Emotion*, New York: Cambridge University Press.

PEACOCKE, ARTHUR R. 1993. *Theology for a Scientific Age: Being and Becoming – Natural and Divine*, 2nd edn., Minneapolis: Fortress Press.

POLKINGHORNE, DONALD. 1988. *Narrative Knowing and the Human Sciences*, Albany, NY: State University of New York Press.

ROSALDO, MICHELLE Z. 1980. *Knowledge and Passion*, New York: Cambridge University Press.

——. 1984. 'Toward an Anthropology of Self and Feeling,' in R. A. Shweder and R. A. Levine (eds), *Culture Theory: Essays on Mind, Self, and Emotion*, New York: Cambridge University Press.

ROSS, LEE D., TERESA M. AMABILE, and JULIA L. STEINMETZ. 1977. 'Social Roles, Social Control, and Biases in Social Perception Processes,' *Journal of Personality and Social Psychology* 35, 485–94.

SAMPSON, EDWARD E. 1988. 'The Debate on Individualism: Indigenous Psychologies of the Individual and Their Role in Personal and Societal Functioning,' *American Psychologist* 3, 15–22.

SCHAFER, ROY. 1976. *A New Language for Psychoanalysis*, New Haven, Conn: Yale University Press.

SEARLE, JOHN R. 1969. *Speech Acts: An Essay on the Philosophy of Language*, New York: Cambridge University Press.

——. 1995. *The Construction of Social Reality*, New York: The Free Press.

SHOTTER, JOHN. 1984. *Social Accountability and Selfhood*, Oxford: Basil Blackwell.

SHWEDER, RICHARD A., and EDMUND J. BOURNE. 1982. 'Does the Concept of the Person Vary Cross-Culturally?,' in A. J. Marsalla and G. White (eds), *Cultural Concepts of Mental Health and Therapy* 97–137, Boston: Reidel.

——, and JOAN G. MILLER. 1985. 'The Social Construction of the Person: How Is It Possible?,' in K. J. Gergen and K. E. Davis (eds), *The Social Construction of the Person* 41–69, New York: Springer-Verlag.

SLUGOSKI, B. R., and G. P. GINSBERG. 1989. 'Ego Identity and Explanatory Speech,' in J. Shotter and K. J. Gergen (eds), *Texts of Identity* 36–55, Newbury Park, Calif.: Sage.

SPENCE, DONALD. 1982. *Narrative Truth and Historical Truth*, New York: W. W. Norton.

TAYLOR, CHARLES. 1989. *Sources of the Self: The Making of Modern Identity*, Carbondale, Ill.: Southern Illinois University Press.

TESKE, JOHN A. 1996. 'The Spiritual Limits of Neuropsychological Life,' *Zygon* 31, 209–34.

——. 1998. 'The Neuroanthropological Fabric of Spirit,' in N. H. Gregersen, M. W. S. Parsons and C. Wassermann (eds), *Studies in Science and Theology*, vol. 5, 163–78, Geneva: Labor et Fides.

——. 1999. 'The Haunting of the Human Spirit,' *Zygon* 34, 307–22.

TETLOCK, PHILIP, and RICHARD BOETTGER. 1989. 'Accountability: A Social Magnifier of the Dilution Effect,' *Journal of Personality and Social Psychology* 57, 388–98.

TILLICH, PAUL. 1957. *Systematic Theology*, Evanston, Ill.: University of Chicago Press.

TOMKINS, SILVAN S. 1979. 'Script Theory: Differential Magnification of Affects,' in H. E. Howe, Jr, and R. A. Dienstbier (eds), *Nebraska Symposium on Motivation 1978*, vol. 26, 201–36, Lincoln, Nebr.: University of Nebraska Press.

VYGOTSKY, LEV S. 1978. *Mind in Society*, Cambridge, Mass.: Harvard University Press.

WINCH, PETER. 1958. *The Idea of a Social Science and Its Relation to Philosophy*, London: Routledge & Kegan Paul.

WITTGENSTEIN, LUDWIG. 1953. *Philosophical Investigations* (trans. G. E. M. Anscombe), New York: Macmillan.

WRIGHT, LAWRENCE. 1993. 'Remembering Satan,' *The New Yorker* I.60–81, II.54–76.

Index

213